THE WRITING ON THE WALL

108 AMERICAN
POEMS OF PROTEST
edited by
Walter Lowenfels , 1847-
comp.

THE
WRiTiNG
ON THE
WaLL

DOUBLEDAY & COMPANY, INC., GARDEN CITY, NEW YORK

Library of Congress Catalog Card Number 69–12187
Compilations Copyright © 1969 by Walter Lowenfels
All Rights Reserved
Printed in the United States of America

Grateful acknowledgment is made to the following publishers, agents, and individuals for permission to use poems under their control:

Atlantic-Little, Brown and Company, for lines from "Poem Issued by Me to Congressmen" from *White Paper* by George Starbuck; copyright © 1966 by George Starbuck. This poem originally appeared in *Poetry*.

A. S. Barnes & Company, Inc., for "April 29th" from *They Look Like Men* by Alexander Bergman.

City Lights Books, for "Hello" by Gregory Corso; copyright © 1958 by Gregory Corso.

E. Clemente & Sons, Publishers, for "When the Cock Crows" from *The Collected Poems of Arturo Giovannitti*.

Dodd, Mead & Company, for lines from *Rendezvous with America* by Melvin Tolson; copyright, 1944, by Dodd, Mead & Company.

Dorothy Durem, for "Award" by Ray Durem.

Mrs. Norma Millay Ellis, for "Justice Denied in Massachusetts" from *Collected Poems* by Edna St. Vincent Millay; copyright 1928, 1955 by Edna St. Vincent Millay and Norma Millay Ellis. Published by Harper & Row, Publishers.

Rachel and Urie Funaroff, for lines from "Bellbuoy" from *Spider and the Clock* by Sol Funaroff.

Harcourt, Brace & World, Inc., for "Pity This Busy Monster, Manunkind," copyright, 1944, by e. e. cummings, from *Poems 1923–1954* by e. e. cummings.

Harper & Row, Publishers, for "Hurrying Away from the Earth" from *The Light Around the Body* by Robert Bly, copyright © 1967 by Robert Bly; "We Real Cool" from *Selected Poems* by Gwendolyn Brooks, copyright © 1959 by Gwendolyn Brooks Blakely; "Incident" from *Color* by Countee Cullen, copyright 1925 by Harper & Brothers, renewed 1953 by Ida M. Cullen; and "To the Powers of Desolation" from *Collected Poems* by Genevieve Taggard, copyright 1938 by Harper & Brothers, renewed 1966 by Kenneth Durant.

My call is the call of battle. I nourish active rebellion.

Walt Whitman

To a 12th Grandchild

Don't stop the scream you got born with.
Resist, resist, and then resist.
    And keep up that occasional smile
        that lights your crib.
You can grow as old as Doctor Du Bois
    but follow your smile-scream syndrome
and you'll reach the Himalayas
    of eternal unrest

WHAT TIME IS IT?

Poetry (or any other art) relates to the question: What time is it? There's no mystery about the answer today. We are all hung up on the hot line between atomic catastrophe and human triumph. "Oh dear! Oh dear!" said the White Rabbit as he looked at his watch, "how late it's getting." That's what our poets are saying in this book.

Ours is a great time to be alive—not because "happy days are here" or coming—but because we are the first generation absolutely certain that tomorrow will not be like today. If it is, our country's tomorrow is heading toward a silent atomic graveyard.

For poets, of course, there will always be a red-hot inferno here and now because things are as they are—not as they should be. That's the theme of this anthology—resistance against the world the way it is.

It is well known that any word is the possibility of a poem and our selection is not designed to substitute for your reading poems about love, spring, and all the other beautiful words. Rather, this book is a guide to one of the major themes that have inspired poets since Chu Yuan wrote his *Song of Everlasting Sorrows* in 300 B.C. The book will achieve its purpose if it sends readers to the Bible to reread the Lamentations of Jeremiah as well as the love songs of Solomon, to Shakespeare's *King Lear*, as well as his *Romeo and Juliet* or his love sonnets, to Sophocles, Euripides, Aristophanes—and so on through the great lovers and haters who have mastered in verse the art of telling it the way it is.

Anthologies of poetry are more widely read today than all but one or two individual poets. This practice can become a dangerous habit. It leaves to others the job of selecting what's good for us to read. Then why am I editing an anthology? (And not only one, this is my fourth or fifth.) It's the other anthologies of modern poems that drive me to it. They all contain good poems, but they don't seem to me for the most part to reflect the direction in which U.S. poetry is moving today.

We are in the greatest upsurge of poems this or any country has known since the T'ang dynasty (China, A.D. 700). How can we account for the high quality and great quantity of new poems since the early fifties? The tensions of being alive in the megaton days have given the language a new dimension. As it becomes "more dangerous to speak, and more impossible to stay silent," (Julian Tuwim), new poems increase by geometrical progression. Now everybody seems to want to say his last words, paint his last pictures, write his last symphony. But the very act of writing it down while we can is a sign of belief in tomorrow.

It is within this over-all framework that poems function today—trying to break out of the strait jacket of literary texts to be part of people's lives.

These poets are not "strange fowl" (as Heine, the great German poet, was once described by a friend), they are craftsmen who have mastered the technique of transforming ordinary prose words into little flashes of lightning to show us the wounded landscape of our time. The raw material of poems is all around all of us. We are all poets really—if only while reading someone else's poems. For the poem comes alive when you read it—otherwise it's dead ink marks on a page. Poems are incubating today not only in spring flowers and beautiful bodies, but in the schools, the streets—wherever you find unrest and uprisings. One of our poems, *Jitterbugging in the Streets,* was written during a street insurrection in Harlem. And several of the poems are by people in their teens or even younger.

In the mid-fifties, Allen Ginsberg, Lawrence Ferlinghetti, and others (once known as the "Beat Poets") suddenly broke through the barrier of the literary elite. They quickly won a wide audience among young people—ten years before any anthologist would include them.

What was the central characteristic of these poets? Protest, anger—not considered "poetry" by many critics. Now the outsiders of a dozen years ago have become contemporary "classics" and new, younger poets are arriving on the scene, many of them found only in little magazines that circulate in the literary underground. One aim of this anthology is to trace a continuity between angry poets of the past and the young poets who are crying out against things today. Thus we include several much earlier poets who seem contemporary today and who have, I think, been undeservedly neglected in recent decades.* But the vast majority of the poems and the impact of the book represent the renaissance that started in the mid-fifties and continues today.

In many countries overseas we are known as "the land of Whitman." We are also the land of the black poet, Claude McKay, who wrote "if we must die, let it not be like hogs/hunted and penned in an inglorious spot . . ./Like men we'll face the murderous, cowardly pack,/Pressed to the wall, dying, but fighting back!"

Most U.S. anthologies suffer from a peculiar color blindness. They give the reader white poetry only. Why do they generally exclude Afro-American verse?

I would say that for one thing it is its national or ethnic quality. Although poets like Mari Evans, or Clarence Major, write about many subjects, they have a special experience as black people in a white country. Thus their work often incorporates a verbal texture that is unique. It has roots not only in the world literary tradition from which white poets take off, but also in the oral tradition of black people—their music, their songs, their special way of communicating with each other. The inclusion of some thirty black or brown or Indian poets in this anthology has been determined not by

* Whitman's poem, *Respondez!*, belongs in this category. Written in 1856, it was later suppressed by Whitman and is not to be found in the usual editions of his *Leaves of Grass*.

color but by what I respond to when "I hear America singing."

Protest is a universal and eternal theme for poets:

It's not that I reject anyone.
But I will not submit to being slaughtered without stating
    where I stand.
I am a victim of the International Geophysical year.
I protest, your honor. It's true I am guilty. But does that
    make so much difference? (W.L.)

That is to say, it's not just tyrants or oppression that poets oppose—they are against the universe, and in their most powerful and passionate outbursts at the human condition, they are at the same time affirming the unique and precious instant that we breathe and live.

Poems are one evidence that we know how to be more than rocks. Our whole history is a living protest against geology. And if it still shows signs of horrors and blood, that's the way tomorrow gets born.

We are entering the unknown world—the future. Science fiction is a joke compared to what we face. Those who have been there in verbal spasms or jazz improvisations have left the scene different from what it was. That's the tough nut for some of us to crack, the unexpected, the jazzman Coltrane who trips you up as you spin the dial because the new music isn't what it was.

We don't need artists to "inspire" humanity. Humanity will find its way ahead via inexorable laws. We are heading toward a humanity who will take those laws for granted and will be asking: "What else, what's the whole story about? What did you see in that kiss or that rose or that barricade you stormed, that nobody else saw?"

We want that inaudible now. Nothing less will do. Poems project the future, they show how it feels to be human in the ice age of an automated world.

ACKNOWLEDGMENTS

To Lillian Lowenfels without whose creativity there are no poems.

To Nan Braymer my devoted collaborator in this as well as all my other books.

To the poets and friends who helped me find and select many of the poems: Art Berger, Ben Botkin, Olga Cabral, Robert Kelly, Thomas McGrath, Felix Pollak, Allen De Loach

To Georgess McHargue of Doubleday & Company for her enthusiastic and creative editing.

To those who typed so faithfully: Claire Gale, Manna Perpelitt, Judith Wiesenfeld.

CONTENTS

III. Orphans

IV. There Must Be a Lone Ranger

V. Justice Denied

VI. *Tape Found in a Bottle*

VII. *Bury Me Not on the Lone Prairie*

VIII. *Which Side Are You On?*

MELVIN TOLSON
From Rendezvous with America

TEMPO PRIMO
The New Negro strides upon the continent
In seven-league boots . . .
The New Negro
Who sprang from the vigor-stout loins
Of Nat Turner, gallows-martyr for Freedom,
Of Joseph Cinquez, Black Moses of the Amistad Mutiny,
Of Frederick Douglass, oracle of the Catholic Man,
Of Sojourner Truth, eye and ear of Lincoln's legions,
Of Harriet Tubman, Saint Bernard of the Underground Rail-
    road.

The New Negro
Breaks the icons of his detractors,
Wipes out the conspiracy of silence,
Speaks to his America . . .

TEMPO DI MARCIA
Out of abysses of Illiteracy,
Through labyrinths of Lies,
Across wastelands of Disease . . .
We Advance!

Out of dead ends of Poverty,
Through wildernesses of Superstition,
Across barricades of Jim Crowism . . .
We advance!
With the Peoples of the World . . .
We advance!

LAWRENCE FERLINGHETTI
From I Am Waiting

I am waiting for my case to come up
and I am waiting
for a rebirth of wonder
and I am waiting for someone
to really discover America
and wail
and I am waiting
for the discovery
of a new symbolic western frontier
and I am waiting
for the American Eagle
to really spread its wings
and straighten up and fly right
and I am waiting
for the Age of Anxiety
to drop dead
and I am waiting
for the war to be fought
which will make the world safe
for anarchy
and I am waiting
for the final withering away
of all governments
and I am perpetually awaiting
a rebirth of wonder

I am waiting for the Second Coming
and I am waiting
for a religious revival
to sweep thru the state of Arizona
and I am waiting
for the Grapes of Wrath to be stored
and I am waiting
for them to prove
that God is really American
and I am seriously waiting . . .
for Aphrodite
to grow live arms
at a final disarmament conference
in a new rebirth of wonder

I am waiting
to get some intimations
of immortality
by recollecting my early childhood
and I am waiting
for the green mornings to come again
youth's dumb green fields come back again
and I am waiting
for some strains of unpremeditated art
to shake my typewriter
and I am waiting to write
the great indelible poem
and I am waiting
for the last long careless rapture
and I am perpetually waiting
for the fleeing lovers on the Grecian Urn
to catch each other up at last
and embrace
and I am awaiting
perpetually and forever
a renaissance of wonder

JOHN SINCLAIR
From Homage to John Coltrane

"John Coltrane can do this for us"

teach us to stand
like men
in the face of the most devas-
tating insensi-
tivity. can touch us
where the hand or mouth or
eye
      can't go. can see. can be
a man. make a love
from centuries of unplumbed music
& a common metal tool
anyone can misuse.
                  can make you think
"of a lot of weird & wonderful things"

    yrself.
        beauty.
      love.

gold & miles
        of trees. elvin
    jones. murdered
  dreams. a—
      pocalypse.
      turtles.

        the moon (&
beyond.
            ornette.
                    grapefruits.
            silver pendulums.

MUSIC

        time.
                screaming,
jumping up & down, moaning
for some strange new
dignity
            before anyone can listen. before
time. before promises,
& lies. before it all collapses
on our heads.

        before it's too late

EZRA POUND
The Rest

O helpless few in my country,
O remnant enslaved!

Artists broken against her,
A-stray, lost in the villages,
Mistrusted, spoken-against,

Lovers of beauty, starved,
Thwarted with systems,
Helpless against the control;

You who cannot wear yourselves out
By persisting to success,
You who can only speak,
Who cannot steel yourselves into reiteration;

You of the finer sense,
Broken against false knowledge,
You who can know at first hand,
Hated, shut in, mistrusted:

Take thought:
I have weathered the storm,
I have beaten out my exile.

KENNETH REXROTH
From Thou Shalt Not Kill

They are murdering all the young men.
For half a century now, every day,
They have hunted them down and killed them.
They are killing them now.
At this minute, all over the world,
They are killing the young men.
They know ten thousand ways to kill them.
Every year they invent new ones.
In the jungles of Africa,
In the marshes of Asia,
In the deserts of Asia,
In slave pens of Siberia,
In the slums of Europe,
In the nightclubs of America,
The murderers are at work.

They are stoning Stephen,*
They are casting him forth from every city in the world.
Under the Welcome sign,
Under the Rotary emblem,
On the highway in the suburbs,
His body lies under the hurling stones.
He was full of faith and power.
He did great wonders among the people.
They could not stand against his wisdom.
They could not bear the spirit with which he spoke.

* Stephen, the first Christian martyr, was stoned to death—Ed.

He cried out in the name
Of the tabernacle of witness in the wilderness.
They were cut to the heart.
They gnashed against him with their teeth.
They cried out with a loud voice.
They stopped their ears.
They ran on him with one accord.
They cast him out of the city and stoned him.
The witnesses laid down their clothes
At the feet of a man whose name was your name—
You.

You are the murderer.
You are killing the young men.
You are broiling Lawrence on his gridiron.†
When you demanded he divulge
The hidden treasures of the spirit,
He showed you the poor.
You set your heart against him.
You seized him and bound him with rage.
You roasted him on a slow fire.
His fat dripped and spurted in the flame.
The smell was sweet to your nose.
He cried out,
"I am cooked on this side,
Turn me over and eat,
You
Eat of my flesh."

You are murdering the young men.
You are shooting Sebastian with arrows.‡
He kept the faithful steadfast under persecution.
First you shot him with arrows.

† Lawrence, an early Christian martyr, brought the poor and sick when
asked to show his treasures, and was condemned to death on the gridiron—Ed.
‡ Sebastian, a Roman discovered to be a Christian, was condemned to be
tied to a tree as a target for Roman archers—Ed.

Then you beat him with rods.
Then you threw him in a sewer.
You fear nothing more than courage.
You who turn away your eyes
At the bravery of the young men.

You,
The hyena with polished face and bow tie,
In the office of a billion dollar
Corporation devoted to service;
The vulture dripping with carrion,
Carefully and carelessly robed in imported tweeds,
Lecturing on the Age of Abundance;
The jackal in double-breasted gabardine,
Barking by remote control,
In the United Nations;
The vampire bat seated at the couch head,
Notebook in hand, toying with his decerebrator;
The autonomous, ambulatory cancer,
The Superego in a thousand uniforms;
You, the finger man of behemoth,
The murderer of the young men. . . .

ISHMAEL REED

sermonette

a poet* was busted by a topless judge
his friends went to morristwn nj & put
black powder on his honah/s doorstop
black powder into his honah/s ear
black powder on his honah/s briefs
tiny dolls into his honah/s mind

by nightfall ye honah could a go go no no
his dog went crazy & ran into a crocodile
his widow fell from a wall &
hanged herself
his daughter was run over by a black man
coming home for the wakes the two boys
skidded into mourning
all the next of kin/s teeth fell out

gimmie dat ol time   religion
        it/s good enough for we

---

* The poet LeRoi Jones was sentenced to two and a half to three years by
a Newark judge—Ed.

TULI KUPFERBERG
Would You Believe?

Break the patterns! Shatter the images! Down icons!
Tune In, Turn On, Drop Out!
Fake games! Your games are fake, boring.
Man was made to change. No single thing abides.
Flow with me! Fast flows the abiding tide.
God in a bottle? But Lord, they *said* you were *everywhere!!*

       * * *

Out of my enthusiasm, out of my love, I have
spoken a poem. Only sometimes do poems change
the world. Sometimes the world changes poems.
Is this the call of the siren? Have I minimized
difficulties? Many will die between the time I
write this & the time you read this.

I only did what I had to.
I will not express fear & death. I will express life & hope.
Someday some youth's vision will spring us full blown into
      Paradise.
Either that or we die.
Come dance with me in Johnson's land!

RAY DUREM
From Award

[A Gold Watch to the FBI Man (who has followed me)
for 25 Years.]

Well, old spy
looks like I
lead you down some pretty blind alleys,
took you on several trips to Mexico,
fishing in the high Sierras,
jazz at the Philharmonic.
You've watched me all your life,
I've clothed your wife,
put your two sons through college,
what good has it done?
Sun keeps rising every morning.
Ever see me buy an Assistant President,
Or close a school?
Or lend money to Somoza?
I bought some afterhours whiskey in L.A.
but the Chief got his pay.
I ain't killed no Koreans,
or fourteen-year-old boys in Mississippi,
neither did I bomb Guatemala,
or lend guns to shoot Algerians.
I admit I took a Negro child
to a white rest room in Texas,
but she was my daughter, only three,
and she had to pee,
and I just didn't know what to do,
would you?

See, I'm so light, it don't seem right
to go to the colored rest room;
my daughter's brown, and folks frown on that in Texas,
I just don't know how to go to the bathroom in the
      free world!

ANONYMOUS
From Back of the Bus
new southern folksong

    If you miss me on the picket line
        And you can't find me nowhere
    Come on over to the city jail
        I'll be rooming over there.

    If you miss me in the freedom fight
        And you can't find me nowhere
    Come on over to the graveyard
        I'll be buried over there.

LENORE KANDEL
From First They Slaughtered the Angels

1.

First they slaughtered the angels
tying their thin white legs with wire cords
and
opening their silk throats with icy knives
They died fluttering their wings like chickens
and their immortal blood wet the burning earth

we watched from underground
from the gravestones, the crypts
chewing our bony fingers . . .
now in the aftermath of morning
we are rolling away the stones from underground, from the
caves
we have widened our peyote-visioned eyes
and rinsed our mouths with last night's wine
we have caulked the holes in our arms with dust and flung
libations at each other's feet
And we shall enter into the streets and walk among them and
do battle
holding our lean and empty hands upraised
we shall pass among the strangers of the world like a
bitter wind
and our blood will melt iron
and our breath will melt steel
we shall stare face to face with naked eyes
and our tears will make earthquakes

and our wailing will cause mountains to rise and the sun to
    halt

THEY SHALL MURDER NO MORE ANGELS!
    not even us

NANCY WILLARD
The Graffiti Poet

I grew up in the schoolrooms of the Dakotas,
I sat by the wood stove and longed for spring.
My desk leaned like a clavichord, stripped of its hammers,
and on it I carved my name, forever and ever,
so the seed of that place should never forget me.
Outside, in their beehive tombs, I could hear
the dead spinning extravagant honey.
I remembered their names and wanted only
that the living remember mine.

I am the invisible student, dead end
of a crowded class. I write and nobody answers.
On the Brooklyn Bridge, I wrote a poem:
the rain washed it away.
On the walls of the Pentagon, I made
My sign; a workman blasted me off like dung.
From the halls of Newark to the shores
of Detroit, I engrave my presence with fire
so the lords of those places may never forget me.

Save me. I can hardly speak. So we pass,
not speaking. In bars where your dreams drink,
I scrawl your name, my name, in a heart
that the morning daily erases.
At Dachau, at Belsen I blazoned my cell
with voices and saw my poem sucked
into a single cry:
throw me a fistful of stars.
I died writing, as the walls fell.

I am lonely. More than any monument,
I want you to see me writing: *I love
you* (or someone), *I live* (or you live).
Canny with rancour, with love, I teach you
to spell, to remember your name
and your epitaphs which are always changing.
Listen to me, stranger, keep me alive.
                    I am you.

ETTORE RELLA
Vital Statistics

Emerson was born in eighteen-three
and died in eighteen-eighty-two;
Hawthorne was born in eighteen-four
and died in eighteen-sixty-four;
Thoreau was born in eighteen-seventeen
and died in eighteen-sixty-two;
Melville was born in eighteen-nineteen
and died in eighteen-ninety-one;
Whitman was born the same year as Melville
but died in eighteen-ninety-two;
Dickinson was born in eighteen-thirty
and died in eighteen-eighty-six;
Mark Twain was born in eighteen-thirty-five
and died way out here in nineteen-ten.

Therefore from eighteen-thirty-five
until eighteen-sixty-two (can you see
what I'm getting at?), for the brief and enchanted
time of twenty-seven years
Emerson, Hawthorne, Thoreau and Melville,
Whitman, Dickinson and Mark Twain
were alive together (can you believe it?)
qualifying the American landscape—

the best damn picnic we ever had
and the music still holds in the ravaged clearing
piled high now with dead automobiles.

WALT WHITMAN
From Respondez!

Respondez! Respondez!

Let every one answer! let those who sleep be waked! let none
     evade!

Must we still go on with our affections and sneaking?

Let me bring this to a close—I pronounce openly for a new
     distribution of roles;

Let that which stood in front go behind! and let that which
     was behind advance to the front and speak;

Let murderers, bigots, fools, unclean persons, offer new
     propositions! . . .

Let the people sprawl with yearning, aimless hands! let their
     tongues be broken! let their eyes be discouraged! let
     none descend into their hearts with the fresh
     lusciousness of love!

(Stifled, O days! O lands! in every public and private
     corruption!

Smother'd in thievery, impotence, shamelessness, mountain-
     high;

Brazen effrontery, scheming, rolling like ocean's waves around
     and upon you, O my days! my lands! . . .)

Let none but infidels be countenanced!

Let the eminence of meanness, treachery, sarcasm, hate, greed,
     indecency, impotence, lust, be taken for granted above
     all! let writers, judges, governments, households,
     religions, philosophies, take such for granted above all!

Let the worst men beget children out of the worst women!

Let the priest still play at immortality!

Let death be inaugurated!

Let nothing remain but the ashes of teachers, artists, moralists, lawyers, and learn'd and polite persons!

Let him who is without my poems be assassinated!

Let the cow, the horse, the camel, the garden bee—let the mudfish, the lobster, the mussel, eel, the sting ray, and the grunting pigfish—let these, and like of these, be put on a perfect equality with man and woman!

Let churches accommodate serpents, vermin, and the corpses of those who have died of the most filthy of diseases!

Let marriage slip down among fools, and be for none but fools!

Let men among themselves talk and think forever obscenely of women! and let women among themselves talk and think obscenely of men!

Let us all, without missing one, be exposed in public, naked, monthly, at the peril of our lives! let our bodies be freely handled and examined by whoever chooses!

Let nothing but copies at second hand be permitted to exist upon the earth!

Let the earth desert God, nor let there ever henceforth be mention'd the name of God!

Let there be no God!

Let there be money, business, imports, exports, custom, authority, precedents, pallor, dyspepsia, smut, ignorance, unbelief! . . .

Let all the men of These States stand aside for a few smouchers! let the few seize on what they choose! let the rest gawk, giggle, starve, obey! . . .

Let insanity still have charge of sanity!

Let books take the place of trees, animals, rivers, clouds!

Let the daub'd portraits of heroes supersede heroes!

Let the manhood of man never take steps after itself!

Let it take steps after eunuchs, and after consumptive and genteel persons!

Let the white person again tread the black person under his heel! (Say! which is trodden under heel, after all?)

Let the reflections of the things of the world be studied in
        mirrors! let the things themselves still continue
        unstudied!
Let a man seek pleasure everywhere except in himself!
Let a woman seek happiness everywhere except in herself!
(What real happiness have you had one single hour through
        your whole life?)
Let the limited years of life do nothing for the limitless years
        of death! (What do you suppose death will do, then?)

LANGSTON HUGHES

Let America Be America Again

Let America be America again.
Let it be the dream it used to be.
Let it be the pioneer on the plain
Seeking a home where he himself is free.

(America never was America to me.)

Let America be the dream the dreamers dreamed—
Let it be that great strong land of love
Where never kings connive or tyrants scheme
That any man be crushed by one above.

(It never was America to me.)

O, let my land be a land where Liberty
Is crowned with no false patriotic wreath,
But opportunity is real, and life is free,
Equality is in the air we breathe.

(There's never been equality for me,
Nor freedom in this "homeland of the free.")

Say who are you that mumbles in the dark?
And who are you that draws your veil across the stars?

I am the poor white, fooled and pushed apart,
I am the Negro bearing slavery's scars.
I am the red man driven from the land,
I am the immigrant clutching the hope I seek—

And finding only the same old stupid plan
Of dog eat dog, of mighty crush the weak.

I am the young man, full of strength and hope,
Tangled in that ancient endless chain
Of profit, power, gain, of grab the land!
Of grab the gold!
Of grab the ways of satisfying need!
Of work the men! Of take the pay!
Of owning everything for one's own greed!

I am the farmer, bondsman to the soil.
I am the worker sold to the machine.
I am the Negro, servant to you all.
I am the people, worried, hungry, mean—
Hungry yet today despite the dream.
Beaten yet today—O, Pioneers!
I am the man who never got ahead,
The poorest worker bartered through the years.

Yet I'm the one who dreamt our basic dream
In that Old World while still a serf of kings.
Who dreamt a dream so strong, so brave, so true,
That even yet its mighty daring sings
In every brick and stone, in every furrow turned
That's made America the land it has become.
O, I'm the man who sailed those early seas
In search of what I meant to be my home—
For I'm the one who left dark Ireland's shore,
And Poland's plain, and England's grassy lea,
And torn from Black Africa's strand I came
To build a "homeland of the free."

The free?

A dream—
Still beckoning to me!

O, let America be America again—
The land that never has been yet—
And yet must be—
The land where every man is free.
The land that's mine—
The poor man's, Indian's, Negro's ME—
Who made America,
Whose sweat and blood, whose faith and pain,
Whose hand at the foundry, whose plow in the rain,
Must bring back our mighty dream again.
Sure, call me any ugly name you choose—
The steel of freedom does not stain.
From those who live like leeches on the people's lives,
We must take back our land again,
America!

O, yes,
I say it plain,
America never was America to me,
And yet I swear this oath—
America will be!
An ever-living seed,
Its dream
Lies deep in the heart of me.

We, the people, must redeem
Our land, the mines, the plants, the rivers,
The mountains and the endless plain—
All, all the stretch of these great green states—
And make America again!

WAIST DEEP IN THE big MUDDY

ALEXANDER BERGMAN
April 29th

Will it be remembered
that this day was beautiful?
That all its history
was not recorded in communiqués,
conflicting headlines,
and the secret archives of chancelleries?
     It was an ideal day for scouting flights
     and strafing enemy concentrations.

Not loud, nor hidden by design,
but still more secret than the plots
and plans that charted ways to death,
were the small, common deeds
of men who made no headlines,
gave no statements to the press,
men who made no choice of war or peace.
     And in the Parliaments the guilty leaders said,
     The whole people are responsible.

Of these the substance of the day was made,
by these the day survived,
on these hope nourished and for these
the final war is fought.

It will be remembered that this day
was beautiful with usual skies,
with constant earth,
with sleep and work and love.
     It was a perfect day for flying kites.

CLARENCE MAJOR
Vietnam #4

a cat said
on the corner

the other day
dig man

how come so many
of us
niggers

are dying over there
in that white
man's war

they say more of us
are dying

than them peckerwoods
& it just
   don't make sense
unless it's true
that the honkeys

are trying to kill us out
with the same stone

they killing them other cats
with

you know, he said
two birds with one stone

HAYDEN CARRUTH
The Event Itself

A curious reticence afflicts my generation, faced with the
     holocaust;
We speak seldom of the event itself, but only of what will
     be lost;
We, having betrayed our fathers and all our silent grandfathers,
     cannot cry out for ourselves, the present and tempest-
     tossed.

But many things and all manner of things will be hurled
In a force like dawnlight breaking, and the billion bagpipes of
     our screams will be skirled
Stupendously month after month, the greatest pain ever known
     in the world.

There will be some instantly indistinguishable from the molten
     stone;
But most will have bleeding, burning, gangrene, the sticking-
     out bone;
Men, women, and little children will be made pregnant of the
     nipping crab whose seed will be universally sown.

In the screaming and wallowing one thought will make each
     eye stare,
And that thought will be the silence pressing down at the
     end of the air,
Soon to smother the last scream forever and everywhere.

For the last man in the world, dying, will not know that he is
     the last,
But many will think it, dying; will think that in all the vast
And vacant universe they are the final consciousness, going
    out, going out, going out, with nothing to know it has
    passed.

X

PETER SEEGER
Waist Deep in the Big Muddy

It was back in nineteen forty-two,
I was part of a good platoon.
We were on maneuvers in Loozianna,
One night by the light of the moon.
 The captain told us to ford a river,
 and that's how it all begun.
 We were knee deep in the Big Muddy,
 but the big fool said to push on.

The sergeant said, Sir, are you sure
This is the best way back to the base?
Sergeant, go on; I've forded this river
Just a mile above this place.
 It'll be a little soggy but just keep slogging
 We'll soon be on dry ground.
 We were waist deep in the Big Muddy
 And the big fool said to push on.

The sergeant said, Sir, with all this equipment
No man'll be able to swim.
Sergeant, don't be a nervous nellie
The captain said to him.
 All we need is a little determination
 Men, follow me, I'll lead on.
 We were neck deep in the Big Muddy
 And the big fool said to push on.

All at once, the moon clouded over
We heard a gurgling cry
A few seconds later, the captain's helmet
Was all that floated by.
    The sergeant said, turn around men
    I'm in charge from now on
    And we just made it out of the Big Muddy
    With the captain dead and gone.

We stripped and dived and found his body
Stuck in the old quicksand.
I guess he didn't know that the water was deeper
Than the place he'd once before been
    Another stream had joined the Big Muddy
    Just a half mile from where we'd gone.
    We were lucky to escape from the Big Muddy
    When the big fool said to push on.

Well, I'm not going to draw any moral,
I'll leave that to yourself
Maybe you're still walking, you're still talking,
And you'd like to keep your health
    But every time I read the papers
    That old feeling comes on:
    We're waste deep in the Big Muddy
    And the Big Fool says to push on.

DENISE LEVERTOV
What Were They Like?

1) Did the people of Viet Nam
   use lanterns of stone?
2) Did they hold ceremonies
   to reverence the opening of buds?
3) Were they inclined to quiet laughter?
4) Did they use bone and ivory,
   jade and silver, for ornament?
5) Had they an epic poem?
6) Did they distinguish between speech and singing?

1) Sir, their light hearts turned to stone.
   It is not remembered whether in gardens
   stone lanterns illumined pleasant ways.
2) Perhaps they gathered once to delight in blossom,
   but after the children were killed
   there were no more buds.
3) Sir, laughter is bitter to the burned mouth.
4) A dream ago, perhaps. Ornament is for joy.
   All the bones were charred.
5) It is not remembered. Remember,
   most were peasants; their life
   was in rice and bamboo.
   When peaceful clouds were reflected in the paddies
   and the water buffalo stepped surely along terraces,
   maybe fathers told their sons old tales.
   When bombs smashed those mirrors
   there was time only to scream.

6) There is no echo yet
   of their speech which was like a song.
   It was reported their singing resembled
   the flight of moths in moonlight.
   Who can say? It is silent now.

ED STONE
How Does My Garden Grow?

Last night I thought I heard the bomb fall
but it was only the death rattle of a cricket.
I went out to see if the bomb had damaged
my vegetable garden (the moles have given
me no peace of mind)—and I met hundreds
of black-clad crickets en route to the cricket
cemetery. Joining them I observed the burial
of their beloved patriarch. Believe me there
wasn't a dry eye in the bunch. This morning
I saw three moles wearing black leg bands
carrying a head of my lettuce out to the
cricket cemetery. Their concept of flowers.
I won't kill any more moles. I must be
getting old. Maybe I'm just nervous.

BARBARA GIBSON
Thinking About the Unthinkable

The killing is unthinkable. Thinking
about killing is unbearable. Babies
are born and are killed and we
think about it. "About it"
is not it, is not enough, is not
unbearable enough, is still
thinkable. Stillborn is enough,
but being born and then killed is more
than enough, is unthinkable. Enough
is enough.
        We are thinking
about the unthinkable, killing.
It is unbearable. We bear
babies and we kill them. The babies
are thinking about us, somewhere where
they are, killed, unborn. They
are thinking that we are dead. Because
we keep thinking and we keep bearing
the unbearable. It is enough.
It is too much to bear. It is
unthinkable. But we kill and
we become dead and we make dead and
we are killed and we think and are thought of
and it is unbearable.
        We do not
want to sink down into despair
but we are. We must not sink down
there but we are there already,
I think. That is why we keep thinking

about the unbearable and bearing
the unthinkable. That is because
the unborn, stillborn, born but killed
babies think ill of us. We cannot stand
their ill will. The force of their thinking
about us is sinking us down into despair,
is drowning us in our guilt.
                              Tell me
how to get out of this, someone.
I need someone to help me get out of this poem,
some baby somewhere perhaps. We need
someone to help us get out of this despair
we are sinking into and out of this thinking thing
we've gotten into and all this unbearability
and out of this poem. Help us
get out of this killing, somebody.

BOB ALLEN
Musical Vietnams

A polyphonic symphony of napalm bombs
   sounds a melody of busted babies
                  gutted mothers
                  decapitated men
Harmonizing bombers in azure skies
   paint paddies below blood red
                  bone white
                  dead blue
The rhythm of clattering M-14s
   reacts with local citizens
                  adding further color
                  to the local scene
This swinging symphony of sound and sight
   is the greatest yet performed by the
                  Great Society
"But who can really dig that jazz
   9000 miles away?"
Don't sweat it man let me clue you in
   There is a combo in Watts
     and a quartet in Harlem
       rehearsing groovy sounds
         for a spectacular jazz blast
               right in your
               back yard

ELIZABETH BARTLETT
The Barren Fig Tree

You should have seen it, Father, the day
they attacked, a day as dark as night,
with clouds of fire both front and rear. They
ran like horses, climbed walls, broke ranks, spied
out of windows, their faces pained, black,
while the earth bled till the moon shone red.
Well, old men have their dreams and young men
their visions, but that day won't come back
until the mountains fall and the hills
bury us, if they are here still.
I've seen green land turn to salt, and worms
rot under clods, while men talk peace terms.

ALLEN GINSBERG

Pentagon Exorcism

"No taxation without representation"

Who represents my body in Pentagon? Who spends
my spirit's billions for war manufacture? Who
levies the majority to exult unwilling in
Bomb roar? *Brainwash!* Mind-fear! Governor's language!
Military-Industrial-Complex President's language?
Corporate voices jabber building Electric Networks
of body-pain, chemical ataxia, physical slavery
to diaphanoid Chinese yellow cosmic-eye movie
hysteria fabricated on my credit? No General
wants to be Devil, others die for his Power
sustaining hurt millions in house security
tuning to images on TV's separate universe
where inferior manhoods burn in black and white forest
villages represented less than myself by magic
Intelligence influence matter-scientist's money
bank telephone war investment Usury Agency
executives jotting from McConnell-Douglas to General
      Dynamics
over smog-shrouded metal-noised treeless cities
patrolled by radio fear with tear gas, businessman!
Go spend your bright billions for this suffering
Pentagon wake from planet-sleep! Apokatastasis!
Spirit Spirit Dance Dance Spirit Spirit Dance!
Transform Pentagon skeleton to maiden-temple O Phantom
Guevara! Om Raksa Raksa Hum Hum Hum Phat, Svaha!
Back back back Anger Control, your self feared
Chaos, suffocation, body death in Capitols caved
with stone Radar sentinels! Central Mind Machine,

Pentagon reverse consciousness! Gaze billions
on man-spirit's Pentacle! Manifest! Magnanimous
reaction to signal Peking isolate space Beings!

Milan, September 29, 1967

GEORGE STARBUCK

From Poem Issued by Me to Congressmen

Mine eyes have seen the glory of hard
                              work at least.
I have kept the bore unpitted and the
                              action greased.
Even when it ain't a fit night out for
                              man or beast.

    Brandenburg, Louisiana!
    New Vienna, Minnesota!
    Venezuela, West Virginia!
    Get outa my back yard.

I have seen at least the star shell and the
                              muzzle flash.
I have sabotaged for glory and a little cash.
I have fought my jammed controls right up
                              until the crash.
What's your story, Mister?

    Macedonia, Nevada!
    Himalaya, Oklahoma!
    Okinawa, Indiana!
    Get outa my back yard.

I have walked my twenty-thousand-mile perimeter.
I have cruised at eighty fathoms and a thousand per.
If I didn't they would get my wife and ravish her.
What's your story, Mister?

South Kamchatka, North Dakota!
Lebanon, South Carolina!
Dutch Guiana, Arizona!
Get outa my back yard.

In the beauty of a moment of camaraderie
With a godforsaken bunch of gooks across the sea,
I shall die to make men safe in my society.
What's your story, Mister?

Guatemala, California!
Anatolia, Nebraska!
Hispaniola, Pennsylvania!
Get outa my back yard.
(You take off your insignia. You seek
cover. Maybe they still come sniping at you.
Maybe the outline of a bloused fatigue
uniform is a recognition pattern.

You take off your insignia. Through white
wildernesses of rock to where white water
spins from the snows, still climbing in a white
silence they cut to ribbons with their chatter,

You take off your insignia. The crest
holds you a moment, meeting, of no color
other than that of sunset, their distressed
and automatic redface compulsive stutter.

You take off your insignia. Escape
is a simple melting into the landscape.)

VERN RUTSALA
News

From miles away
the whole
city glows with
the supper

of neon
it eats every
night. And the war
burns on, the glow

over the city
fed by that
white heat. Our
candlelit meals,

flecks of gold
in the wine,
feed on that glow;
our easy talk

in warm rooms
draws heat
from that fire;
our long rocket

cars are fueled
by that glow.
And faces relax,
their tensions

siphoned off
by pictures
of burned houses,
poisoned rice,

dead children,
clubbed prisoners.
They like it.
Lines disappear,

they grow young
on it. They like
it. It tastes
good to them.

They like it.
They like it.
They like it.
They like it.

FELIX POLLAK
Speaking: The Hero

I did not want to go.
They inducted me.

I did not want to die.
They called me yellow.

I tried to run away.
They court-martialed me.

I did not shoot.
They said I had no guts.

They ordered the attack.
A shrapnel tore my guts.

I cried in pain.
They carried me to safety.

In safety I died.
They blew taps over me.

They crossed out my name
and buried me under a cross.

They made a speech in my hometown
I was unable to call them liars.

They said I gave my life.
I had struggled to keep it.

They said I set an example.
I had tried to run.

They said they were proud of me.
I had been ashamed of them.

They said my mother should also be proud.
My mother cried.

I wanted to live.
They called me a coward.

I died a coward.
They call me a hero.

MARGE PIERCY

The Peaceable Kingdom

*In front of a painting by Edward Hicks
(1780–1849) in the Brooklyn Museum*

Creamcheese babies square and downy as bolsters
in nursery clothing nestle among
curly lions and soft lowing cattle,
a wolf of scythe and ashes, a bear smiling in sleep.
The paw of a leopard with spots and eyes of headlights
rests near calf and vanilla child.
In the background under the yellow autumn tree
Indians and settlers sign a fair treaty.
The mist of dream cools the lake.

On the first floor of the museum Indian remains
are artfully displayed. Today is August 6th.
Man eats man with sauces of newsprint.
Peace has no country, only ravines in the mind.
Johnson in toga. Senators posture and crawl.
The rhetoric of the republic gilds empire.

The vision of that kingdom of satisfaction
where all bellies are round with sweet grasses
cools my face with pleasure,
though I have eaten five of those animals.
We are all fat and busy as maggots.
All the rich flat black land
the wide swirlmarked browngreen rivers
leafy wheat baking tawny, corn's silky spikes,
sun bright kettles of steel and crackling wires turn into
infinite shining weapons that scorch the earth.
The pride of our hive
packed into hoards of murderous sleek bombs.

We glitter and spark righteousness.
We are blinding as a new car in the sunshine.
Gasoline rains from our fluffy clouds.
Everywhere our evil froths, polluting the waters—
in what stream on what mountain do you miss
the telltale redbrown sludge and rim of suds?

Peace: the word lies like a smooth slimy turd
on the tongues of politicians ordering
the sweet flesh seared on the staring bone.
Guilt is added to the municipal water,
guilt is deposited in the marrow and teeth.
In my name they are stealing from people with nothing
their slim bodies. When did I hire these assassins?

My mild friend no longer paints doors and mirrors.
On her walls the screams of burning children
coagulate the paints in loud harsh clots.
The mathematician with his webspangled language
of shadow and substance half finished
sits in an attic playing the flute all summer
for fear of his own brain, for fear the baroque
arabesque will turn under his government
into a knife that pierces the breasts of women.
Five A.M. in Brooklyn: night all over my country.
Watch the smoke of guilt drift up out of dreams.

When did I hire these killers? One day in anger,
in seaslime hatred at the wobbly duplicity of flesh?
eating steak in a suave restaurant, did I give the sign?
sweating like a melon in bed did I murmur consent?
But once, once I signed a loyalty oath in Indiana.
Now in my name blood burns like oil day and night.

This nation is founded on blood like a city on swamps
yet its dream has been beautiful and sometimes just
that now grows brutal and heavy as a burned-out star.

EDGAR LEE MASTERS
Harry Wilmans

I was just turned twenty-one,
And Henry Phipps, the Sunday-school superintendent,
Made a speech in Bindle's Opera House.
"The honor of the flag must be upheld," he said,
"Whether it be assailed by a barbarous tribe of Tagalogs
Or the greatest power in Europe."
And we cheered and cheered the speech and the flag
     he waved
As he spoke.
And I went to the war in spite of my father,
And followed the flag till I saw it raised
By our camp in a rice field near Manila,
And all of us cheered and cheered it.
But there were flies and poisonous things;
And there was the deadly water,
And the cruel heat,
And the sickening, putrid food;
And the smell of the trench just back of the tents
Where the soldiers went to empty themselves;
And there were the whores who followed us, full of
     syphilis;
And beastly acts between ourselves or alone,
With bullying, hatred, degradation among us,
And days of loathing and nights of fear
To the hour of the charge through the steaming swamp,
Following the flag,
Till I fell with a scream, shot through the guts.
Now there's a flag over me in Spoon River!
A flag! A flag!

SAMUEL HAZO
To a Commencement of Scoundrels

My boys, they lied to you.
The world by definition stinks
of Cain, no matter what
your teachers told you. Heroes
and the fools of God may rise
like accidental green
on gray saharas, but the sand
stays smotheringly near.

Deny me if you can. Already
you are turning into personnel,
manpower, figures on a list
of earners, voters, prayers,
soldiers, payers, sums
of population tamed with forms:
last name, middle name, first name—
telephone—date of birth—

home address—age—hobbies—
experience. Tell them the truth.
Your name is legion. You
are aged a million. Tell
them that. Say you breathe
between appointments: first day,
last day. The rest is no
one's business. Boys, the time

is prime for prophecy.
Books break down their bookends.
Paintings burst their frames.
The world is more than reason's
peanut. Homer sang it real.
Goya painted it, and Shakespeare
staged it for the pelting rinds
of every groundling of the Globe.

Wake up! Tonight the lions
hunt in Kenya. They
can eat a man. Rockets
are spearing through the sky.
They can blast a man to nothing.
Rumors prowl like rebellions.
They can knife a man. No one
survives for long, my boys.

Flesh is always in season,
lusted after, gunned, grenaded,
tabulated through machines,
incinerated, beaten to applause,
anesthetized, autopsied, mourned.
The blood of Troy beats on
in Goya's paintings and the truce
of Lear. Reason yourselves

to that, my buckaroos,
before you march for God,
country and siss-boom-bah!
You won't, of course. Your schooling
left you trained to serve
like cocksure Paul before
God's lightning smashed
him from his saddle. So—

I wish you what I wish
myself: hard questions
and the nights to answer them,
the grace of disappointment
and the right to seem the fool
for justice. That's enough.
Cowards might ask for more.
Heroes have died for less.

DON GORDON
The Kimono

Celebrate the season of the death
    of the city.
Celebrate the woman in the newsreel,
    the print of her kimono
Burned in her back. Celebrate the bamboo
    leaves, the folded fans.

Exhibit A, formerly a person, was born
    as the white plant bloomed;
She is the night dream of the spectator,
    incised on the lidless eye;
Woman without face or name that is known
    lives in my house.

Weigh her, measure her, peer for children
in her clouded history; check with Geiger counters
in the click of the doomed leaves and fans.

Lost in events the beauty and the grace
    of women;
Ended the age of natural love as the
    bomb bay opened
On the burned shoulders: she is now
    the memorable one.

From the nightmare to the eye
from the eye to the house
from the house to the heart
enter the dimension of love:

women of Hiroshima
be merciful to the merciless!

DELMORE SCHWARTZ
Someone Is Harshly Coughing as Before

Someone is harshly coughing on the next floor,
Sudden excitement catching the flesh of his throat:
Who is the sick one?
                    Who will knock at the door,
Ask what is wrong and sweetly pay attention,
The shy withdrawal of the sensitive face
Embarrassing both, but double shame is tender
We will mind our ignorant business, keep our place.

But it is God, who has caught cold again,
Wandering helplessly in the world once more,
Now he is phthisic, and he is, poor Keats
(Pardon, O Father, unknowable Dear, this word,
Only the cartoon is lucid, only the curse is heard),
Longing for Eden, afraid of the coming war.

The past, a giant shadow like the twilight,
The moving street on which the autos slide,
The buildings' heights, like broken teeth,
Repeat necessity on every side,
The age requires death and is not denied,
He has come as a young man to be hanged once more!

Another mystery must be crucified,
Another exile bare his complex care,
Another spent head spill its wine, before
(When smoke in silence curves
                                from every fallen side)

Pity and Peace return, padding the broken floor
With heavy feet.
                    Their linen hands will hide
In the stupid opiate the exhausted war.

JOHN BEECHER
Wisdom of the Abbot Macarius I

Said he: "I can no longer sanction
    any war for any purpose
        under God's sun or stars"
And they put him in chains

Said he: "I can no longer sanction
    any war for any purpose
        under God's sun or stars"
And they showed him the scaffold

Said he: "I can no longer sanction
    any war for any purpose
        under God's sun or stars"
And they laid his head on the block

Said he: "I can no longer sanction
    any war for any purpose
        under God's sun or stars"
And the ax fell

Whereupon the multitude fell silent
    thinking
        well
He could be right

RANDY RHODY
Orphans

born in the comet tail of a war
infants nursed on the gory remnants of a holocaust
urchins digging in the rabble of a crumbled humanity
seeking to erect life in spite of all
    the destruction of love
growing up in the midst of rebuilt brick piles
    and rubbish heaps
anxious for the triumphant day
    of no more trouble
    and no more self-denial
waiting not much longer for elusive humanity

we are the war babies
suckled on disease
weaned on disease
raised on disease
smothered in disease
now we are sick of disease
we have had our fill of the bigoted memories
    of bleeding shame
    and disgusting self-degradation

we are the war babies
crying
we demand a cure
we are through with filling our
    stomachs and lives with nausea
and if that is our only food
we will fast

and we will starve
we will die
but we will not die grovelling
    in the wretched humiliation
    of gorging on our own excrement
we are sick of the taste in our mouths

we are the war babies
born in shame we will definitely not
    die in shame
we are sick but we will cease to vomit
    on one another
we have been betrayed
    by the fathers who fed us in sickness
    but we shall not be bitter
no we will not spray our problems
    in the faces of each other
we will love to find the cure
we are the infants
    who can trust no parents
we
are the war babies

CHRISTOPHER BURSK
Adjust, Adjust

I was born committing suicide,
holding my breath; they had to drag me kicking
out of this damp garage, this airtight inside,
the gases I struggled back to
until the doctors slapped me alive
and shouted: survive, survive.

After Hiroshima, turning four,
I battered my head at the master bedroom door;
every night I dreamt I was a child burning at that town
        dump
at the world's edge, Japan;
and every night my father yelled: be brave,
behave, behave.

I ripped his set of Plato at eight,
the year my mother was put away at Boston State,
and war was fought in some darkness called Korea;
all winter, I played dead in the corner
while my teachers clapped:
adapt, adapt.

Grandmother took me in till I was ten;
with her best silver carving knife I locked her with me
in the den, all night, clinging to her bathrobe, demanding
to cut our wrists in a lovers' pact;
her only promise I could secure
was: endure, endure.

I threw tantrums into eleven;
I couldn't sleep; McCarthy lashed out at reds in the
        nightmares
where he held me witness; they nailed grandmother up for
        heaven,
that year; I pounded my fingers bloody on the pews
while the minister spit:
submit, submit.

I counted my bones, waiting to be dead;
at thirteen, an invalid in this nursing home, my bed,
I watched the homemakers of Arkansas rail at Negro girls
between commercials, curse the first graders
whom they tried to storm,
shrieking: conform, conform.

At fifteen, in South Station where I ran away,
every week, I bedded down on papers inksmudged with
        the blood
of freedom fighters, left in heaps in Hungary to decay,
while old men rubbed against my thighs,
lulling me to them with the hum
of: succumb, succumb.

I couldn't. Even with sleeping pills,
razor blades, I couldn't. While the U.S. played chicken
in the hills with atom bombs, I gave up my body like
        sixteen years
of hardened clay to be molded slippery
under the touch of my girl's hand and thigh
while she moaned all night: comply, comply.

Why couldn't I? When the world lapsed wide
and elastic into too much, too bright space when Kennedy
        died
and the roads wore bald; and the yards stretched between
        houses,

and the towns gleamed like chrome, I drove into walls,
day after day while the police barked:
obey, obey.

Can't you bleed? Coward, can't you die
while wrists are cut, throats slit, those children, all
  suicides,
are gassed in Vietnam; at twenty-four can you only cry
while men shoot themselves to death
in the DMZ, and your analyst coughs; you must
adjust, adjust.

THOMAS MCGRATH
Gone Away Blues

Sirs, when you are in your last extremity,
When your admirals are drowning in the grass-green sea,
When your generals are preparing the total catastrophe—
I just want you to know how you can*not* count on me.

    I have ridden to hounds through my ancestral hall,
    I have picked the eternal crocus on the ultimate hill,
    I have fallen through the window of the highest
          room,
    But don't ask me to help you 'cause I never will.

Sirs, when you move that map-pin how many souls must
         dance?
I don't think all those soldiers have died by happenstance.
The inscrutable look on your scrutable face I can read at
         a glance—
And I'm cutting out of here at the first chance.

    I have been wounded climbing the second stair,
    I have crossed the ocean in the hull of a live wire,
    I have eaten the asphodel of the dark side of the
          moon,
    But you can call me all day and I just won't hear.

O patriotic mister with your big ear to the ground,
Sweet old curly scientist wiring the birds for sound,
O lady with the Steuben glass heart and your heels so rich
         and round—
I'll send you a picture postcard from somewhere I can't
         be found.

I have discovered the grammar of the Public Good,
I have invented a language that *can* be understood,
I have found the map of where the body is hid,
And I won't be caught dead in *your* neighborhood.

O hygienic inventor of the bomb that's so clean,
O lily-white Senator from East Turnip Green,
O celestial mechanic of the money machine—
I'm going someplace where *nobody* makes your scene.

    Good-by, good-by, good-by,
    Adios, Au 'voir, so long,
    Sayonara, Dosvedanya, ciao,
    By-by, by-by, by-by.

SONIA SANCHEZ
Poem for 8th Graders

Look at me 8th
grade.
     i am black
beautiful. i have a
man who looks at
my face and smiles.
on my face
are black warriors
riding in ships
of slavery;
        on my face
           is malcolm
               spitting his metal seeds
on a country of sheep;
on my face
       are young eyes
breathing in black crusts.
            look at us
8th grade
     we are black
beautiful and our black
ness sings out
        while america wanders
dumb with her wet bowels.

GWENDOLYN BROOKS
We Real Cool

The Pool Players.
Seven at the Golden Shovel.

We real cool. We
Left school. We

Lurk late. We
Strike straight. We

Sing sin. We
Thin gin. We

Jazz June. We
Die soon.

JANE STEMBRIDGE
The Children

The children of the world who're wanting
ice-cream cones are filling up the streets,
stopping tanks

talk a little softer Mom
I can't hear

listen to the lollipops
dance

bubblegum candy canes peanut butter cups
the stickiness of city streets
is slowing murder down

let us build a government
made of gingerbread

we'll give it all
away

let us clear the hill of everything
except the cherry trees

and let the senate meet
inside an orchard
and adjourn

open up the hydrants wash the city down
the drain

a meadow makes a miracle for butterflies
to paint

an ocean makes a rockehorse for little fish
to ride

a rainbow makes an underpass
to purple worlds

I want a president who's nine years old
to organize the country from his treehouse
home

playing hookey every day
so that everyone will say
just exactly what he needs
just exactly where he bleeds
very clearly what he hears
and what monster face he fears
and what plan he has in mind
and what wounds he has to bind
and what friends he has to find
and whatever in the lonely world it takes

for him to do his total thing
let him make his way
to that

immediately

HYACINTHE HILL
Rebels from Fairy Tales

We are the frogs who will not turn to princes.
We will not change our green and slippery skin
for one so lily-pale and plain, so smooth
it seems to have no grain. We will not leave
our leap, our spring, accordion. We have
seen ourselves in puddles, and we like
our grin. Men are so up and down, so thin
they look like walking trees. Their knees seem stiff,
and we have seen men shooting hares and deer.
They're queer . . . they even war with one another!
They've stretched too far from earth and natural things
for us to admire. We prefer to lie
close to the water looking at the sky
reflected; contemplating how the sun,
Great Rana, can thrust his yellow, webbed foot
through all the elements in a giant jump;
can poke the bottom of the brook; warm
the stumps for us to sit upon; and heat
our backs. Men have forgotten to relax.
They bring their noisy boxes, and the blare
insults the air. We cannot hear the cheer
of crickets, nor our own dear booming chugs.
Frogs wouldn't even eat men's legs.
We scorn their warm, dry princesses. We're proud
of our own bug-eyed brides with bouncing strides.
Keep your magic. We are not such fools.
Here is the ball without a claim on it.
We may begin from the same tadpoles, but
we've thought a bit, and will not turn to men.

WILLIAM WANTLING
Rune for the Disenchanted

What if:

—In a moment of pure terror I refused the call of Beauty
  by stuffing bank notes in my ear?

—In a moment of pure intuition I bit and scratched my
  cat and sought to learn her secret?

—In a moment of pure compassion I refused to hate my
  enemy?

—In a moment of pure vision I awoke from out my
  lonely dream?

—In a moment of pure understanding I howled with
  laughter which never ceased, flinging roses all about
      me?

—In a moment of pure decision I called our game a
  draw?

—In a moment of pure sophistication I refused to play
  my role and pierced my ears with seashells?

—In a moment of pure inspiration I began to love my
  dream of life, and thus resumed my game and role?

ART BERGER
From No Generation Gap

When I was a young man
coming up
my elders told me
the future belongs to the youth
and I believed it
              yes I did
and I worked to change the world.

One time 'round was spent finding out
that all they were doing
              was putting me on;
but an Aquarius rocks and all I need
              is just one more time.

Now I am a bridge
              and not an island
cross me if you can
and find yourself
in flesh that is your own.

Show me a stone
I'll show you sand
show me a boy
I'll show you a man
find me tomorrow
yesterday is a creep. . . .

Turn on a river
if you dig my sound

and tune in the signal
of tomorrow,
drop out of calamity
for change is the name
of the game.

On an island where days
are made of sulphur
and nights of vaseline,
show me a sphincter
and I'll show you a stone
show me yesterday
I'll show you a ghost
today is a creep but
                    tomorrow is boss.

SOL FUNAROFF
Bellbuoy

I am that exile
from a future time,
from shores of freedom
I may never know,
who hears, sounding in the surf,
tidings from the lips of waves
that meet and kiss
in submarine gardens
of a new Atlantis
where gold-colored fishes
paint the green gloom.

And where the cracked heart of the world
sobs through great fissures
whose boiling hells
raise volcanic fires
and tears of stone,
in huge convulsions,
waterspouts and steam,
eternity gives birth,
and from its watery womb
emerges a continent
from the slime of oceans.

Then tossed by seas rebellious and proud
with stormy syllables in mass cascades
my songs are sung.

RUTH LISA SCHECHTER
Bound Together

Stumbling
in our own curriculum
we learned the love of
letting go, paid for
the daydream of you
standing up to be
heard. Escaping. Stabbed
in teen-age mirrors of wishing
your face was not. Nametapes
unspooled summer to summer. Over
and over the linens folded
with the nightmares of brothers
murdered and the women
longed for. On vista-
vision screens, the unattainable
dream swung
in traction. Books piled up, on
IQ ladders of past and present
history. You marched from
classroom pictures to streets named
after American presidents, you walked
into towns of blind
obedience. Bruised by the burning
question flung like acid in
the eye. How can you be a student in
a society that refuses to learn?

RENÉE RESENDEZ

From The Trouble Is . . .

The trouble is i
know that i am in
a cave
Chained to that all-
American myth
        Everyone must go to college

Chained so that i
may not turn to
discover
Seeing only shadows
images of reality
But not real at all

A tragicomedy played
by puppets
manipulated by someone
who knows what is good
for me
Not what i am good for

My identity seems
lost i have no name
Attached to my face
an IBM number filed
in that glorified
library
        San José State

Directed through halls
listening not hearing
memorizing not remembering
studying not learning
              wondering
                     why?

College does not give
me an education
i cannot learn about truths
i have to live them
i cannot be kept from lies
i see them

Occupying a space
taking notes faster faster
everyone writing
heads down words words
Any questions?
                No time
i want to know
what is really
going on
i want to understand
Bombs for peace
Aggression security
War?
              why not

Memorize the Constitution
recite the Preamble
learn the Bill of Rights
the meaning of democracy
Turn around and see
                Selma, Alabama

Pity the poor in India
the starving Chinese
Increase Foreign Aid
give to CARE
Face the light
                    "U.S. War on Poverty"

But i am safe in my
cave secure protected
Vietnam weapons Kill
Remember Korea Hiroshima
forget it
            play it cool

It is my future
it is their future
Put an end to the mistakes
before they put an end
to us . . .

DILYS LAING
Forgive Me

Forgive me for neglecting to show you
      that the world is evil.
I had hoped your innocence would find
      it good
and teach me what I know to be untrue.

Forgive me for leaving you open to
      persistent heartbreak
instead of breaking your bright heart
      with medicinal blows.
I had hoped your eyes would be stars
dispelling darkness wherever you
      looked

Forgive me for a love that has delivered you
unwarned to treachery. Now I confess
      that the world,
more beautiful for your presence, was
      not fine enough
to warrant my summoning you into it.
      My beloved.

TIM HALL
Come Here, My Friends

Come here, my friends,
we have something to do together.
What we do will be our own
and we will do it when we want to do it.

It is not true that our lives & troubles have
        been performed before
and everything to do has already been done.
Who has lived my life before?
Who has lived ours?
Produce him, bankers, leaders, fathers!
Show him to us.

And who has lived the year 1967 before?
Who has walked down this particular street where
        I go walking
in this particular dappled afternoon sunlight
        on a January 2nd and thought these thoughts
        before?
Produce him, liars, produce him now!

And who has taken the same open road that we have,
        friends, hitchhiking
into the deceptive sunlight of 1967 and experienced
        our peculiar
total fears of nuclear radiance and country clubs,
and felt the great doors closing on our
        childlike dreams?
Produce him! Produce him! or we'll know.

They will tell us that this has all been done
    before,
there is nothing new under the sun,
and our shouts are useless.
And we will ask: Why is it, then, that you have
    no solutions?
Why did you leave us with this?

—You see, we haven't been alive as long as you.
We haven't got used to it. It doesn't make sense.
    It looks wrong.
All we have is our eyes, and when they ask you
    a question, fathers,
why do you get so nervous?

Friends, these words for our enemies are harsh—
    and insufficient.
We must name them, and our heroes, and ourselves.
We must make a revolution.
So come with me.
We have something to do together.

BERT LEE

Photograph: Mother and Father: 1930

I have a wrought-iron father
And a mother pale as the work of a lampshade.
When nineteen and thirty caught them in a lens
They were just married and already strangers.

Now my father keeps to himself and union meetings
And dresses as I think a mayor might dress.
He sees the world as billiard-table green
Where people meet and rebound
With the petty click of pool balls.
My mother keeps to herself and, humming,
Dresses with a sense of faded gingham.
She muses how youth once filled the light
Like the shadow of a failing moth.

Memory tells me of the many times
We were three in a room, trapped
By the all-constricting walls of a summer shower.
While water on the window glass painted the walls
With long beards of light. We did not even struggle
In the incredibly wordless wires
Of the raining afternoon, like three
Lugubrious fish snared together in a net of tension,
Each gasping for the small breath of recognition.
I was forced to cry out with the silence of a butler:
Mother. Father. If you can hear me
(Though miles and years have made you deaf)
Remember that a shadow is nothing but a lie
And a mirror is where our shadows put on flesh.

JOHN GILL
From Spring Malediction

Oh Gentlemen Gentlemen don't worry
I leave you this stinking corpse of a college
where the administration has you on your knees
where the Dean the fattest maggot of all
chases everyone who runs in fear of exposure
maggots together turned over caught wiggling
where the Chairman of the department is a bull dragging his
       chain
where titles and privileges shut off open discussion
where worth is not worth without a degree
and beware and cross yourself if you're a popular teacher
it means you're a fraud not the real dull thing
where students bog through the mud of the effort of thinking
where the President too is a bully and uses his thumb
where the tide of hate back-biting and gall rises higher
where a teacher cannot be a man unless he's a willing woman
where . . . but why should I sing this damn school anyway!
I'll gather my poems praise my good fortune spit and leave.

DAVID IGNATOW
Bothering Me at Last

Where is my mother?
Has she gone to the store for food,
or is she in the cellar shoveling coal
into the furnace to keep the house warm?
Or is she on her knees scrubbing the floor?
I thought I saw her in bed
holding a hand to her heart, her mouth open:
"I can't breathe, son. Take me to a hospital."
I looked for her in the cellar.
I looked for her in bed, and found her in her coffin,
bothering me at last.

GREGORY CORSO
Hello . . .

It is disastrous to be a wounded deer.
I'm the most wounded, wolves stalk,
and I have my failures, too.
My flesh is caught on the Inevitable Hook!
As a child I saw many things I did not want to be.
Am I the person I did not want to be?
That talks-to-himself person?
Am I he who, on museum steps, sleeps on his side?
Do I wear the cloth of a man who has failed?
Am I the loony man?
In the great serenade of things,
        am I the most cancelled passage?

THOMAS MERTON
Advice to a Young Prophet

Keep away, son, these lakes are salt. These flowers
eat insects. Here private lunatics
Yell and skip in a very dry country.

Or where some haywire monument
Some badfaced daddy of fear
Commands an unintelligent rite.

To dance on the unlucky mountain,
To dance they go, and shake the sin
Out of their feet and hands,

Frenzied until the sudden night
Falls very quiet, and magic sin
Creeps, secret, back again.

Badlands echo with omens of ruin:
Seven are very satisfied, regaining possession:
(Bring a little mescaline, you'll get along!)

There's something in your bones,
There's someone dirty in your critical skin,
There's a tradition in your cruel misdirected finger
Which you must obey, and scribble in the hot sand:

"Let everybody come and attend
Where lights and airs are fixed
To teach and entertain. O watch the sandy people
Hopping in the naked bull's-eye,

"Shake the wildness out of their limbs,
Try to make peace like John in skins
Elijah in the timid air
or Anthony in tombs:

"Pluck the imaginary trigger, brothers.
Shoot the devil: he'll be back again!"

America needs these fatal friends
Of God and country, to grovel in mystical ashes,
Pretty big prophets whose words don't burn,
Fighting the strenuous imago all day long.

Only these lunatics (O happy chance)
Only these are sent. Only this anemic thunder
Grumbles on the salt flats, in rainless night:

O go home, brother, go home!
The devil's back again,
And magic Hell is swallowing flies.

DOUGLAS BLAZEK
Chicago Kid Winters

Chicago was a small boy once
that grew up with winters
in playgrounds
where children discovered the world
through marbles
& everything was a hundred feet high
& streets were plowed by the enemy
which we fought with snowballs
because we wanted everything
to be icicle & snow &
people wouldn't be able to get to work
& business would stop &
politics would stop & everyone would
be in a snowsuit like Jack London.

MILLEA KENIN
Untitled Poem

Can you see our way home
past the glass walls
that hem in the grey canyons of the city?

    No. I see only our weary faces
    reflected in a thousand panes of glass—
    where someone threw a stone and broke a window
    beyond its random jaws I see darkness.

Can you see friendly lights in windows
anywhere in the dim wake of battles
stretching behind us—and ahead?

    I see the chasms on the road ahead
    I see our enemies have lit the way
    with fiery children.

Yes, but can't you see their hands beckon?

    I see only dead leaves that twist and shrivel
    as flame outlines their veins—
    and blasted walls around dead lots
    where no live things can grow in the cinders—
    I see our time explode around us.
    Where in the future is our homeland?

Can't you see the gardens up ahead
where children play in the long grass?
Their roots are in us—we give them a home
even as we are broken, even as we fall.

JACK LINDEMAN
Trying for Solitude

If I walk on my hands
　　who will follow the prints of my shoes
　　　　on the blue beach of the sky?
Upright I am easily trailed.
I carry a gong
　　　　　　(like a cow)
　　round my neck.
The noise of my tongue
　　　　　　　　as I contemplate hunger
　　is enough to attract a small crowd.
I enter a room like the buzz of a fly
　　and a gamut of hands seeks to slap me to death.
In the wide open air
　　I am burned by the sun or the wind
　　　　as I drag with my eyes
　　　　　　　　　　every building & tree.
Someone intrudes
　　thru every locked door
　　　　I have latched for a thought.
No mind of my own,
　　but a hall in a skull
　　　　where the audience harangues
　　　　　　from a thousand podiums.
If I race towards the woods
　　the trees become people
　　　　and the birds mere chattering verbs.
By the creek
　　the trout
　　　　　　(in a mischievous mood)
　　　　advise me against my own will.

My guests are abundant
                        bearing breezes & suns.
In the house where I dream
    there's a marathon waltz of the dead.
        A stampede of spiders & mice
            protests inside walls.
A jet in the sky
    makes tracks thru my ears.
My hounds
            (whether imagined or real)
    inflate every sound with a howl.
Behind the gloom of my face
    I am constantly guessing
        a clamor unnamed.
The wounds which silence would heal
    are incurably bruised.
The radio's trained on my head
                        like a bombsight.
The cat is meowing for milk,
while the dog that is crunching a bone
    is climbing the stairs of my spine.

ELINOR WYLIE
Let No Charitable Hope

Now let no charitable hope
Confuse my mind with images
Of eagle and of antelope:
I am in nature none of these.

I was, being human, born alone;
I am, being woman, hard beset;
I live by squeezing from a stone
The little nourishment I get.

In masks outrageous and austere
The years go by in single file;
But none has merited my fear,
And none has quite escaped my smile.

MARGARET RANDALL
From Retracing Paul Blackburn's Transit

he says we are beggars
and i say
when it comes to love we are orphans we are
all misplaced or displaced persons from
another war

examining
our hands in such a position
wondering
how did this get to be that and why
how did it come so far or turn
climb
when it comes to love we are all orphans
we are all that old woman slightly deaf and
too old to be riding a bicycle . . .

LEROI JONES
There Must Be a Lone Ranger!!!

but this also
is part of my charm.
A maudlin nostalgia
that comes on
like terrible thoughts about death.

How dumb to be sentimental about anything
To call it love
& cry pathetically
into the long black handkerchief
of the years.

> "Look for you yesterday
> Here you come today
> Your mouth wide open
> But what you got to say?"

-part of my charm

old envious   blues feeling
ticking like   a big cobblestone clock

I hear the reel running out
the spectators are impatient for popcorn:
It was only a selected short subject
F. Scott Charon
will soon be glad-handing me
like a legionnaire

My silver bullets all gone
My black mask trampled in the dust

& Tonto way off in the hills
moaning like Bessie Smith.

D. A. LEVY
the bells of the Cherokee ponies

i thought they were
wind chimes
in the streets at night

with my young eyes
i looked to the east
and the distant ringing
of ghost ponies
rose from the ground

Ponies Ponies Ponies

i looked to the east
seeking buddhas to
justify those bells
weeping in the darkness

*The Underground Horses
are rising*

Cherokee, Delaware, Huron
we will return your land to you

the young horses
will return your land to you
to purify the land
with their tears

The Underground Horses
are rising
to tell their fathers

"In the streets at night
the bells of Cherokee ponies
are weeping."

DONALD JUSTICE
Counting the Mad

This one was put in a jacket,
This one was sent home,
This one was given bread and meat
But would eat none,
And this one cried No No No No
All day long.

This one looked at the window
As though it were a wall,
This one saw things that were not there,
This one things that were,
And this one cried No No No No
All day long.

This one thought himself a bird,
This one a dog,
And this one thought himself a man,
An ordinary man,
And cried and cried No No No No
All day long.

MARI EVANS
Stretchin' Out

i
am going to rise
en masse
from Inner City
                    sick
                        of newyork ghettos
                    chicago tenements
                l a's slums
weary
        of exhausted lands
        sagging privies
        saying yessuh yessah
        yes SIR
        in an assortment
        of geographical dialects i
have seen my last
broken down plantation
even from a
distance
        i
will load all my books
in '50 Chevy pickups '53
Fords fly United and '66
caddys i
            have packed in
            the old man and the old lady and
            wiped the children's noses

I'm tired
of hand me downs
shut me ups
pin me ins
keep me outs
messing me over have
just had it
baby
from
you . . .
i'm
gonna spread out
over America
intrude
my proud blackness
all
over the place
I have wrested wheat fields
from the forests
turned rivers
from their courses
leveled mountains
at a word
festooned the land with
bridges
gemlike
on filaments of steel
moved
glistening towers of Babel in place
sweated a whole
civilization
now
I'm
gonna breathe fire
through flaming nostrils BURN
a place for
me

in the skyscrapers and the
schoolrooms on the green
lawns and the white
beaches
                    i'm
gonna wear the robes and
sit on the benches
make the rules and make
the arrests say
who can and who
can't
            baby you don't stand
            a
            chance
i'm
    gonna put black angels
    in all the books and a black
    Christchild in Mary's arms i'm
    gonna make black bunnies black
    fairies black santas black
    nursery rhymes and
                            black
    ice cream
                    i'm
gonna make it a
    crime
        to be anything BUT black
        pass the coppertone
gonna make white
a twentyfourhour
lifetime
J.O.B.
            an' when all the coppertone's gone . . . ?

LEO CONNELLAN
This Scenery

I said to my friend. "But I marched with you
in a garland of rosaries where death choked on his meal of
    us.
My heart was your heart at the roadside of slaughter."

My friend said to me, "But you are whitey. No armband
of identity, no photograph of us
arm in arm pictured together
will mean a thing in the hour of our hot bloods."

"With tire irons to smash out your treacherous brains.
a razor for your throat. Knives to give your belly button a
    brother.
We are coming to cut you out of us."

"No!" I cried to my friend. "This cannot be. This is not so!
I will not part with my life. You will have to spring
from behind me where I cannot see the stab."

"You do not deserve to be faced like a man," he said.
"You never once treated us as men. I think that is why
we will cut you out of us like Parasites."

"No!" I cried. "I personally am innocent."

"It cannot come to rivers of blood
on the Avenue of Americas with heads looking at each other
like fish in the *mea culpa* of carelessness."

"Count your pigeons of peace, Poet," he said.
"For the next time you turn your head it may not be on
   your shoulders."

JULIUS LESTER
Us

For so long
We looked into mirrors and hated what we saw
For so long
We did not dance to the rhythms of our Gods
but writhed on the cross with christ,
drank his blood and were thankful.
For so long
We proclaimed with pride "Je suis français"
Our black skins glistening
and white teeth shining.
For so long
hot combs burned our hair
and our breasts were cinched and hidden from sight.
For so long
we knew not ourselves
or each other
For so long
We saluted a flag not our own
For so long
We sang My Country 'Tis of Thee
For so long
We died in wars not our own.

But
We are reclaiming our
selves
and
Tomorrow
and

Tomorrow
and
Tomorrow
will
undulate
vibrate
and
dance
to the beat of our hearts.

If I am my   If I am my
self,   self
I have no fear.   I cannot be destroyed.

e. e. cummings

Pity This Busy Monster, Manunkind

pity this busy monster,manunkind,

not. Progress is a comfortable disease:
your victim(death and life safely beyond)

plays with the bigness of his littleness
—electrons deify one razorblade
into a mountainrange;lenses extend

unwish through curving wherewhen till unwish
returns on its unself.
                              A world of made
is not a world of born—pity poor flesh

and trees,poor stars and stones,but never this
fine specimen of hypermagical

ultraomnipotence. We doctors know
a hopeless case if—listen:there's a hell
of a good universe next door;let's go.

ROBERT HAYDEN
Frederick Douglass

When it is finally ours, this freedom, this liberty, this beautiful
and terrible thing, needful to man as air,
usable as earth; when it belongs at last to all,
when it is truly instinct, brain matter, diastole, systole,
reflex action; when it is finally won; when it is more
than the gaudy mumbo jumbo of politicians:
this man, this Douglass, this former slave, this Negro
beaten to his knees, exiled, visioning a world
where none is lonely, none hunted, alien,
this man, superb in love and logic, this man
shall be remembered. Oh not with statues' rhetoric,
not with legends and poems and wreaths of bronze alone,
but with the lives grown out of his life, the lives
fleshing his dream of the beautiful needful thing.

COUNTEE CULLEN
Incident

Once riding in old Baltimore,
Heart-filled, head-filled with glee,
I saw a Baltimorean
Keep looking straight at me.

Now I was eight and very small,
And he was no whit bigger,
And so I smiled, but he poked out
His tongue, and called me, "Nigger."

I saw the whole of Baltimore
From May until December;
Of all the things that happened there
That's all that I remember.

KENNETH PATCHEN
Before the Bells of This New Year Ring

In the shape of this night, in the still fall
      of snow, Father
In all that is defenseless and lost, even as
      the lives of your children
In everything that moves tonight, the trolleys
      and the lovers, Father
In the great hush of fields, in the ugly noise
      of our cities
In this frosty gaze of stars, in those trenches
      where the slain are, Father
In all this wide land waiting, in the great liners
      pitching toy-like upon the shroud-cold sea
In all that has been said honestly, in all that is
      petty and mean at this hour, Father
In all that is good and lovely, in every house
      where sham and hatred are
In the name of those who wait without hope, in the
      sound of angry voices, Father
Before the bells ring, O before this tiny moment
      has become swollen with the grief of a world
Before it becomes as guilt-soiled and hideous as the
      lives of your children, Father
O there is this high clean singing in the air
O forever this sorrowful human face in eternity's window
And there are other bells that we would ring, Father
O there are other bells that we could ring!

KENNETH FEARING
X Minus X

Even when your friend, the radio, is still; even when her dream,
   the magazine, is finished; even when his life, the ticker,
   is silent; even when their destiny, the boulevard, is bare;
And after that paradise, the dance-hall, is closed; after that
   theater, the clinic, is dark,

Still there will be your desire, and hers, and his hopes and
   theirs,
Your laughter, their laughter,
Your curse and his curse, her reward and their reward, their
   dismay and his dismay and her dismay and yours—

Even when your enemy, the collector, is dead; even when your
counsellor, the salesman, is sleeping; even when your
sweetheart, the movie queen, has spoken; even when your
friend, the magnate, is gone.

KIRBY CONGDON
Television-Movie

The monster is loose.
This is an emergency area.
Leave your homes.
There is no time
to gather your belongings.
The highways are jammed,
the trains, derailed.
The planes have crashed
and the bridges are collapsing.
There is no escape.

Aunt Harriet has fallen down,
trying to escape.
The baby is hysterical.
The radio's broken.
The neighbors are gone.
Susie forgot her doll.
I can't find the insurance papers.
The monster has knocked over
the Tower of London.
The Empire State Building
is breaking in half.
Everyone is drowning
in Times Square.

In Tokyo
all the poor people
have fallen into a crevasse
which is now closing up,

even on United States citizens.
The ship's piano is rolling
across the ballroom floor.
The cargo is crushing the coolies.
The Army is out of ammunition.
The President has declared
a national state of affairs.
The almanacs were wrong.
The computers were in error.
Where will it all end?

The baby has stopped crying.
You hold her now; I'm tired.
Aunt Harriet wants to stay
one more week.
I can't say no. You tell her.
The radio repairman will come for sure
—if he can make it.
The neighbors said it's too loud.
Fix Susie's doll; the squeak's gone.
The insurance papers
are in the bottom left-hand drawer
right where you put them.
If they're not there,
keep looking.
Will you get paid tomorrow?
Did you mail my letter?
Did you set the alarm?

The monster is dead.
He is never coming back.
And if he does come,
someone will kill it.
And we will go on
just like always.
There is no escape.

CHIEF JOSEPH*
Surrender Speech

I am tired of fighting. Our chiefs are killed. Looking Glass is dead. Toohulsote is dead. The old men are all dead. It is the young men who say no and yes. He who led the young men is dead. It is cold and we have no blankets. The little children are freezing to death. My people, some of them, have run away to the hills and have no blankets, no food. No one knows where they are—perhaps they are freezing to death. I want to have time to look for my children and see how many of them I can find. Maybe I shall find them among the dead. Hear me, my chiefs, I am tired. My heart is sad and sick. From where the sun now stands I will fight no more forever.

* Chief Joseph of the Nez Percé tribe of the Northwest led his people for 1300 miles, battling constantly against superior numbers and weapons. At the border of Canada he was trapped by soldiers and made a courageous battle. Though he made an honorable surrender, his people were sent to Oklahoma where most of them died of heat and heartbreak—Ed.

PETER LA FARGE
Vision of a Past Warrior

I have within me such a dream of pain
That all my silver horseman hopes rust still,
Beyond quicksilver mountains,
On the plain,
The buffalo are gone,
None left to kill,

I see the plains grow blackened with that dawn,
No robes for winter warmth
No meat to eat,
The ghost white buffalos' medicine gone,
No hope for Indians then,
I see defeat.

Then there will be changes to another way,
We will fight battles that are legends long.
But of all our glory
None will stay,
Who will remember
That I sang this song.

STAN STEINER

But, the Africans Walked at Night

But, the Africans walked at night
to Lukachukai
to Tohatchi
to Chinle
in the sacred groves of graves of the peach trees
of Kit Carson,
                the father,
of death.

But, the Africans walked at night
succoring the Earth Mother.

But, the Africans walked at night
the lawyers of Ibo and Kikuyu
wondering where are the warrior
sons.

        Come to feast!
        on unleavened bread
        and governmental
        beasts
                to eat
        tribal fables
        mouthed by TV
        tubes full of
        Last Suppers
        of Cheeseburgers—

But, the Africans walked at night
black as Christs
shrouded
in whiteskinned
business suits of cellophane and aluminum foil
under the moon
of the coyote.

But, the Africans walked at night
in Italian shoes.

But, the Africans walked at night
through dark light
to uranium women
in unlit hogans
who welcomed them blindly
to the way of beauty.

But, the Africans walked at night
medicine bags and stone balls
in their attaché cases.

>Where the warriors
>lie in motels
>of the Navajos
>eyeing redhanded
>knives of yellow
>butter eaters
>the blunted spears
>of the eunuched
>Indians—

But, the Africans walked at night
wondering where
John Wayne was hiding
his red cosmetics—
why Gary Cooper shot
Pocahontas—

why
the warriors of Jeff Chandler
washed their wounds white
with detergents

But, the Africans walked at night
to wickiups with beautyrest beds.

But, the Africans walked at night
to exercise
tours of diplomacy
with the State
departmentalized guides who dreamt of reddest sex
frozen in ice cream cones of blackest secrets.

But, the Africans walked at night
four hundred miles
of years of death
marched to wars
across the deserts
of history to be buried
with unborn Indians
in concentration camps
of the Army of Christ.

But, the Africans walked at night
disguised as one million dead Indians, yelling,
Uruhu!

CALVIN C. HERNTON

From Jitterbugging in the Streets

There will be no holy man crying out this year
No seer, no trumpeter, no George Fox walking
    barefoot up and down the hot land
The only messiah we shall see this year
Staggers
To and fro
On the Lower East Side
Being laughed at by housewives in Edsel
    automobiles who teach their daughters the
    fun of deriding a terror belched up from
    the scatological asphalt of America
Talking to himself

An unshaven idiot
A senile derelict
A black nigger
Laughter and scorn on the lips of Edsel
    automobiles instructing the populace to
    love God, be kind to puppies and the
    Chase Manhattan National Bank

Because of this there will be no Fourth of July
    this year
No shouting, no popping of firecrackers, no
    celebrating, no parade
But the rage of a hopeless people
Jitterbugging
In the streets

Jacksonville, Florida
Birmingham, Atlanta, Rochester, Bedford-
Stuyvesant, Jersey City, Chicago,
Jackson, Mississippi, Harlem New York—
Watts, L.A.
Jiggerbugging
    in
    the streets
To ten thousand rounds of ammunition
To water hoses, electric prods, phallic sticks,
    hound-dogs, black boots stepping in soft
    places of the body—
Venom is in the mouth of Christian housewives,
    smart young Italians, old Scandinavians in
    Yorkville, suntanned suburban organization
    men, clerks and construction workers, poor
    white trash and gunhappy cops everywhere
"Why don't we kill all the niggers.
Not one or two
But every damn black one of them. Niggers will do
    anything.
I better never catch a nigger messing with my wife,
And most of all never with my daughter! Aughter
    grab 'em and ship every black clean out of
    the country . . . Aughter just line 'em up and
    mow 'em down
Machine Gun Fire!" . . .

No Holy man shall cry out upon the black ghetto
    this year
No trombonist
The only messiah we will know this year is a
bullet in the belly
    of a Harlem youth shot down by a coward
    crouched behind an outlaw's badge—
Mississippi
Georgia

Tennessee, Alabama
Your mother your father your brothers, sisters,
    wives and daughters
Up and down the hot land
There is a specter haunting America
Spitfire of clubs, pistols, shotguns, and the
Missing
Mutilated
Murdered
Bodies of relatives and loved ones
Be the only Santa Claus niggers will remember
    this year
Be the only Jesus Christ born this year
    curled out dead on the pavement, torso
    floating the bottom of a lake
Being laughed at by housewives in Edsel
    automobiles

You say there are four gates to the ghetto
Make your own bed hard that is where you have got
To lay
You say there is violence in Harlem, niggers
    run amuck perpetrating crimes against
    property, looting stores, breaking windows,
    flinging beer bottles at officers of the law . . .
TERROR is in Harlem
A GENOCIDE so blatant
Every third child will do the junky-nod in the
    whore-scented night before semen leaps
    from his loins
A FEAR so constant
Black men crawl the pavement as if they were
    snakes, and snakes turn to sticks that beat
    the heads of those who try to stand up—
And Fourth of July comes with the blasting bullet
    in the belly of a teen-ager
Against which no Holy man, no Christian housewife

In Edsel Automobile
Will cry out this year

   Jitterbugging
      in
     the streets!

LESLIE WOOLF HEDLEY
Chant for All the People on Earth

Not to forget not to ever forget so long as you live so long
as you love so long as you breathe eat wash walk think see
feel read touch laugh not to forget not to ever forget so long
as you know the meaning of freedom of what lonely nights
are to torn lovers so long as you retain the soul heart of a
man so long as you resemble man in any way in any shape
not to forget not to ever forget for many have already forgotten
many have always planned to forget fire fear death murder
injustice hunger gas graves for they have already forgotten
and want you to forget but do not forget our beloved species
not to forget not to ever forget for as long as you live carry it
with you let us see it recognize it in each other's face and
eyes taste it with each bite of bread each time we shake
hands or use words for as long as we live not to forget what
happened to six million Jews to living beings who looked just
as we look men people children girls women young old good
bad evil profound foolish vain happy unhappy sane insane
mean grand joyous all dead gone buried burned not to forget
not to ever forget for as long as you live for the earth will
never be the same again for each shred of sand cries with
their cries and our lungs are full of their dying sounds for god
was killed in each of them for in order to live as men we must
not forget for if they are forgotten O if they are forgotten forget me also destroy me also burn my books my memory
and may everything I have ever said or done or written may
it be destroyed to nothing may I become less than nothing
for then I do not want even one memory of me left alive
on cold killing earth for life would have no honor for to be
called a man would be an insult—

WORTH LONG
Safari

COME with me
on a safari
into the teeming
jungle darkness
of a black soul
searching for
itself

trek with me
thru these vast
congos

arkansas alabama
mississippi
can you follow me

DEALER
SIGN in a
mississippi
junkyard

we
buy
burnt
bodies

MILLEN BRAND
Local Light

Lightning is local.
First from its pool of cloud
coiled like a serpent,
it flicks its tongue here and there
toward the ground.
First that round
of coiled cloud over a neighborhood,
and then one or a few
hot fangs following the tongue.
At Pat Giagnocavo's, up the lane,
is a tree notched with the heat
that passed its heart and burned
out along a chain to a goat
and notched her heart too.
At Pennsburg,
two baseball players shared
a single blazing strike. Summer flies
north and in Vermont the writhing folds
bite down a tree
in a small cemetery where
thunder dies into the grass.
In Minnesota, a lake of darkening sky
floats over a reflecting lake
and lets down a shine of yellow hair
toward the Mississippi, the father.
Now the clouds coil in the air
high above Sangre de Cristo
in New Mexico, above Chimayo,
glowing red in the evening

with the blood of Christ. The Jemez Canyon
in shadow catches the flashes
against the cliffs. At this altitude,
eight thousand feet, the fang of heat
touches the moisture in a tree,
turning it to steam, and simply
blows the tree up.
A fire may start in the duff
of long-needled ponderosa pine,
smouldering two days, damped down by the rain,
then break out its living flag.
In California, the infrequent storms
signal like canopies shaken
and gleaming along the seams of noon.
A hiss of light covers the jacaranda
and stops where the banana tree wavers
in its earthen socket. Uphill,
the decomposed granite brightens,
mimicking gold, and rolls with the boats
of live oak leaves. In Pennsylvania,
fire is immediate.
Two miles from Pat Giagnocavo's tree,
the snake's bite startled a barn
and the flames roared into the rain,
eating all the wood, leaving
perfectly vertical stone walls
as clean as ideas of walls.
Hard to think, in sunlight,
that pools of fire and death
wait in the sky, an igneous dream
man makes deliberate
with his own fangs.

YURI SUHL
The Permanent Delegate

My name is Jew.
  I come from the land of skeleton.
They beat me in Berlin,
    tortured me in Warsaw,
      shot me in Lublin
And I am still here—the ash of my bones
  a glowing monument, a fiery headstone.

I am the scorched hair of a virgin's bright curls
  smoothed and patted by anxious hands
I am a maddened mother's futile tears
  soothing in vain a hundred anguished hurts.

I am the spasm of a body convulsed in flames,
  the crumbling of a skeleton,
the boiling of blood, shriveling of flesh,
  smouldering ash of six million—
ashes of body, of brain, of vision, of work—
  ashes of genius and dreams,
    ashes of God's master stroke—Man.

Count the limbs, gentlemen—
  match them if you can in pairs.
    It can't be done.
For I am one ghost of six million.
Out of all the ashes I have become one
And the dream lies broken and spit on.

I am here to tell you, gentlemen
   it's a lie—the world is not yet Hitler-free.
Millions see it, condemn it,
   cry out my pain and warn you.

But you are moved like a granite statue
   by the prick of a pin.
Therefore I have come,
   uninvited, unwelcome
     bringing a message
from the land of skeleton.

I am grafting my ash to your souls.
I am hanging my dreams around your necks.
I am blotting out the sun from your day
             with my shadow.
I am tearing the quiet of your night
             with the shrieks of my tortures.
I will beat at your conscience
   with the hands of a million dead children and
I will pick at your brains
             with my maggots
Yea, though you split the atom to infinity
   you will see my face before your eyes.
I sit at all the round tables
At every conference I am a delegate,
my credentials signed by six million
   from the land of skeleton
and you will never get rid of me
   until the world is Hitler-free.

(translated from the Yiddish by Max Rosenfeld
and Walter Lowenfels)

RAYMOND PATTERSON
At That Moment

When they shot Malcolm Little* down
On the stage of the Audubon Ballroom,
When his life ran out through bullet holes
(Like the people running out when the murder began)
His blood soaked the floor
One drop found a crack through the stark
Pounding thunder—slipped under the stage and began
Its journey: burrowed through concrete into the cellar,
Dropped down darkness, exploding like quicksilver
Pellets of light, panicking rats, paralyzing cockroaches—
Tunneled through rubble and wrecks of foundations,
The rocks that buttress the bowels of the city, flowed
Into pipes and powerlines, the mains and cables of the city:
A thousand fiery seeds.

At that moment,
Those who drank water where he entered . . .
Those who cooked food where he passed . . .
Those who burned light while he listened . . .
Those who were talking as he went, knew he was water
Running out of faucets, gas running out of jets, power
Running out of sockets, meaning running along taut wires—
To the hungers of their living. It was said
Whole slums of clotted Harlem plumbing groaned
And sundered free that day, and disconnected gas and light
Went on and on and on . . .

* Malcolm Little took the name Malcolm X when he became a Muslim. He converted to orthodox Islam, believing in the brotherhood of all men. Malcolm X was shot in the Ballroom in 1965—Ed.

They rushed his riddled body on a stretcher
To the hospital. But the police were too late.
It had already happened.

BARTOLOMEO VANZETTI
Last Speech to the Court

I have talk a great deal of myself but I even forgot to name Sacco.* Sacco too is a worker from his boyhood, a skilled worker lover of work, with a good job and pay, a good and lovely wife, two beautiful children and a neat little home at the verge of a wood, near a brook. Sacco is a heart, a faith, a character, a man; a man lover of nature and of mankind. A man who gave all, who sacrifice all to the cause of Liberty and to his love for mankind; money, rest, mundane ambitions, his own wife, his children, himself and his own life. Sacco has never dreamt to steal, never to assassinate. He and I have never brought a morsel of bread to our mouths, from our childhood to today—which has not been gained by the sweat of our brows. Never.

Oh, yes, I may be more witful, as some have put it, I am a better babbler than he is, but many, many times in hearing his heartful voice ringing a faith sublime, in considering his supreme sacrifice, remembering his heroism I felt small small at the presence of his greatness and found myself compelled to fight back from my throat to not weep before him—this man called thief and assassin and doomed. But Sacco's name will live in the hearts of the people and in their gratitude when Katzmann's and your bones will be dispersed by time, when your name, his name, your laws, institutions, and your false god

* Sacco and Vanzetti, Italian immigrants, were tried in 1921 for two murders and found guilty. The controversial verdict was disputed by millions throughout the world, who felt the men had not received a fair trial because of their radical affiliations. A retrial was denied and Sacco and Vanzetti were executed in 1927, maintaining their innocence—Ed.

are but a dim rememoring of a cursed past in which man was wolf to the man . . .

If it had not been for these thing, I might have live out my life talking at street corners to scorning men. I might have die, unmarked, unknown, a failure. Now we are not a failure. This is our career and our triumph. Never in our full life could we hope to do such work for tolerance, for joostice, for man's onderstanding of man as now we do by accident. Our words— our lives—our pains—nothing! The taking of our lives—lives of a good shoemaker and a poor fish-peddler—all! That last moment belongs to us—that agony is our triumph.

EDNA ST. VINCENT MILLAY
Justice Denied in Massachusetts

Let us abandon then our gardens and go home
And sit in the sitting-room.
Shall the larkspur blossom or the corn grow under this cloud?
Sour to the fruitful seed
Is the cold earth under this cloud,
Fostering quack and weed, we have marched upon but cannot
      conquer;
We have bent the blades of our hoes against the stalks of them.

Let us go home, and sit in the sitting-room.
Not in our day
Shall the cloud go over and the sun rise as before,
Beneficent upon us
Out of the glittering bay,
And the warm winds be blown inward from the sea
Moving the blades of corn
With a peaceful sound.
Forlorn, forlorn,
Stands the blue hay-rack by the empty mow.
And the petals drop to the ground,
Leaving the tree unfruited.
The sun that warmed our stooping backs and withered the
      weed uprooted—
We shall not feel it again.
We shall die in darkness, and be buried in the rain.

What from the splendid dead
We have inherited—
Furrows sweet to the grain, and the weed subdued—

See now the slug and the mildew plunder.
Evil does overwhelm
The larkspur and the corn;
We have seen them go under.

Let us sit here, sit still,
Here in the sitting-room until we die;
At the step of Death on the walk, rise and go;
Leaving to our children's children this beautiful doorway,
And this elm,
And a blighted earth to till
With a broken hoe.*

* Edna St. Vincent Millay wrote *Justice Denied in Massachusetts* during
the aftermath of the Sacco-Vanzetti trial—Ed.

ANONYMOUS
The Death of Jesse James

It was on a Wednesday night, the moon was shining bright,
    They robbed the Glendale train.
And the people they did say, for many miles away,
    'Twas the outlaws Frank and Jesse James.

Jesse had a wife to mourn all her life,
    The children they were brave.
'Twas a dirty little coward shot Mister Howard,
    And laid Jesse James in his grave.

It was Robert Ford, the dirty little coward,
    I wonder how he does feel,
For he ate of Jesse's bread and he slept in Jesse's bed,
    Then he laid Jesse James in his grave.

It was his brother Frank that robbed the Gallatin bank,
    And carried the money from the town.
It was in this very place that they had a little race,
    For they shot Captain Sheets to the ground.

They went to the crossing not very far from there,
    And there they did the same;
And the agent on his knees he delivered up the keys
    To the outlaws Frank and Jesse James.

It was on a Saturday night, Jesse was at home
    Talking to his family brave,
When the thief and the coward, little Robert Ford
    Laid Jesse James in his grave.

How people held their breath when they heard of Jesse's death,
   And wondered how he ever came to die.
'Twas one of the gang, dirty Robert Ford,
   That shot Jesse James on the sly.

Jesse went to his rest with his hand on his breast.
   The devil will be upon his knee.
He was born one day in the county of Clay,
   And came from a solitary race.

CLAUDE MCKAY
If We Must Die

If we must die, let it not be like hogs
Hunted and penned in an inglorious spot,
While around us bark the mad and hungry dogs,
Making their mock at our accursed lot.
If we must die, O let us nobly die,
So that our precious blood may not be shed
In vain; then even the monsters we defy
Shall be constrained to honor us though dead!
O kinsmen! we must meet the common foe!
Though far outnumbered let us show us brave,
And for their thousand blows deal one deathblow!
What though before us lies the open grave?
Like men we'll face the murderous, cowardly pack,
Pressed to the wall, dying, but fighting back!

CHARLES BUKOWSKI
The Day I Kicked a Bankroll Out the Window

and, I said, you can take your rich aunts and uncles
and grandfathers and fathers
and all their lousy oil
and their seven lakes
and their wild turkey
and buffalo
and the whole state of Texas
meaning your crow-blasts
and your Saturday night boardwalks,
and your 2-bit library
and your crooked councilmen
and your pansy artists—
you can take all these
and your weekly newspaper
and your famous tornadoes
and your filthy floods
and all your yowling cats
and your subscription to *Life*,
and shove them, baby,
shove them.
I can handle a pick and ax again (I think)
and I can pick up
25 bucks for a 4-rounder (maybe);
sure, I'm 38
but a little dye can pinch the gray
out of my hair;
and I can still write a poem (sometimes),
don't forget that, and even if
they don't pay off,

it's better than waiting for death and oil,
and shooting wild turkey
and waiting for the world to begin.
all right, bum, she said,
get out.

what? I said.

get out. you've thrown your last tantrum.
I'm tired of your damned tantrums:
you're always acting like a
character
in an O'Neill play.

but I'm different, baby,
I can't help it.

you're different, all right!
God, how different!
don't slam
the door
when you leave.

but, baby, I *love* your
money!
you never once said
you loved me!

what do you want
a liar or a
lover?

you're neither; out, bum,
out!

. . . but baby!

go back to O'Neill!

I went to the door,
softly closed it and walked away,
thinking: all they want
is a wooden Indian
to say yes and no
and stand over the fire and
not raise too much hell;
but you're getting to be
an old man, kiddo:
next time play it closer
to the
vest.

KAY BOYLE
A Poem of Love

The day you told me you had a bank account
Of inestimable proportions, too great
For balancing in any cheque-book,
More multitudinous than the loose silver of the Milky Way,
I entered without genuflection the crypt, the bank-vault,
Of the forest, trod moss softer than folding money,
At the cashier's window asked for dandelion heads
To hoard for their coarse gold. With this currency
I have acquired a palm tree here, across the fence,
Beyond the Inca daisies which, according to prophecy,
Were transformed to golden rods by the commandment
Of an oracle whose dark voice bade the descendants of the
   Sun God
To move northward in search of buzzard-dollars, double eagles
    dough.

Being an entire sunset away, you cannot see this palm tree.
It is luxuriant as a peacock's tail, rainbowed by mist
In the early morning, emerald by starlight. It is not lanky
   like a giraffe.
Nor is it parched for speech. Hundreds of birds talk in its
   sixteen storeys.
One day you will race the sun across
America and say: "Why didn't you tell me
About this palm tree that you bought on credit?"
And I will answer: "I told you once when we awoke,
But you have forgotten. Its roots have opened
A savings account in the floating capital of sand that no worm
   riddles,
Somewhere under the invested asphalt of this marginal soil."

At night,
In the tentative wind, it talks your drowsy lingo,
Its palm feathers whispering of earthquake fluctuations.
I do not know on what stock exchange I bid for it, or
What dividends it should pay, or not pay, annually,
But only that it is gold-edged at sunrise, and that
Its mint par of international exchange is love.

The Parted Lovers
(*From the Amerindian*)

TRANSLATED BY JOHN READE

I

The Man Sings

My parents think they can separate me
    from the girl I love;
We have vowed to love each other while
    we live.
Their commands are vain: we shall see
    each other while the world lasts.
Yes! let them say or do what they like;
    we shall see each other while the rocks
    stand.

MURIEL RUKEYSER
Effort at Speech Between Two People

: Speak to me.   Take my hand.   What are you
        now?
I will tell you all.   I will conceal nothing.
When I was three, a little child read a story about a rabbit
who died, in the story, and I crawled under a chair
a pink rabbit : it was my birthday, and a candle
burnt a sore spot on my finger, and I was told to be happy.

: Oh, grow to know me.   I am not happy.   I will
        be open:
Now I am thinking of white sails against a sky like music,
like glad horns blowing, and birds tilting, and an arm about
        me.
There was one I loved, who wanted to live, sailing.

: Speak to me   Take my hand.   What are you
        now?
When I was nine, I was fruitily sentimental,
fluid : and my widowed aunt played Chopin,
and I bent my head on the painted woodwork, and wept.
I want now to be close to you.   I would
link the minutes of my days close, somehow, to your days.

: I am not happy.   I will be open.
I have liked lamps in evening corners, and quiet poems.
There has been fear in my life.   Sometimes I speculate
On what a tragedy his life was, really.

: Take my hand.   Fist my mind in your hand.
        What are you now?
When I was fourteen, I had dreams of suicide,
and I stood at a steep window, at sunset, hoping toward
        death   :
if the light had not melted clouds and plains to beauty,
if light had not transformed that day, I would have leapt.
I am unhappy.   I am lonely.   Speak to me.

: I will be open.   I think he never loved me:
he loved the bright beaches, the little lips of foam
that ride small waves, he loved the veer of gulls:
he said with a gay mouth: I love you.   Grow to know
        me.

: What are you now?   If we could touch one another,
if these our separate entities could come to grips,
clenched like a Chinese puzzle. . . . yesterday
I stood in a crowded street that was live with people,
and no one spoke a word, and the morning shone.
Everyone silent, moving. . . . Take my hand.   Speak
        to me.

WALTER LOWENFELS
For a Hemiplegic

Flowers in the ward
    smell of aspirin, and days
when I loved you like peonies
    and hyacinths and fields
        of daisies . . . fade out.
I love you like a hospital,
    like a wheel chair,
like the hemiplegics
        floating in the pool;
like the young head nurse
    walkless from polio
smiling from her chair:
    your wife
will be walking by herself soon.

Let's get a bulldozer,
plough up every street we ever lived,
    begin all over from scratch,
as if it were the first day
    we met, and you were lame
but I never noticed
    because you were so much you
and did everything your own way
    anyhow.
Believe me it's not all gloomy,
    like when you're half-paralyzed,
and showering is an agony
    on a hard chair.

We can always rely
        on doing it together—
            You hold the shower rail
and I hold you,
        and what love
            can be purer or cleaner
than going into the shower
        hugging each other?
            Just to stand up
and get soaped
        clean to the end,
so happy you don't have to
        wash alone in that cold
hospital chair.
        So, as I said,
            it's not all gloomy—
just a question of balance.
        I love you,
even though all I say is,
        "please pass the soap."

OLGA CABRAL

Electronic Tape Found in a Bottle

If this small human testament
completes its odyssey
clears the curtains of fiery meteors
crosses the rages of magnetic storms
rides free of hydrogen whirlwinds
falls through coalsack eternities
lands smoothly on the Milky Way
glides along its lightband
to the shores of an unknown planet
in an unknown star-continent
to be found and wonderingly
pondered held in your hands—
this message was meant for you.

Be advised that I lived on
a small green ball in the suburbs
of an unremarkable sun
that had begun to run down.
Our race was a sun-people
but died of diseases called wars.
To you out there in star cities
with your libraries, fountains
or you who are still making it
through ice ages of ignorance—
whoever or whatever you are
here is earth's final message:
I love you I love you I love you.

There is nothing more to say
there is nothing better here
and nothing in all the spiraling nebulae
was as frail or as mighty as this.

Lament of a Man for His Son
(*From the Amerindian*)

TRANSLATED BY MARY AUSTIN

Son, my son!

I will go up to the mountain
And there I will light a fire
To the feet of my son's spirit,
And there will I lament him;
Saying,
O my son,
What is my life to me, now you are departed!

Son, my son,
In the deep earth
We softly laid thee in a Chief's robe,
In a warrior's gear.
Surely there,
In the spirit land
Thy deeds attend thee!
Surely,
The corn comes to the ear again!

But I, here,
I am the stalk that the seed-gatherers
Descrying empty, afar, left standing.
Son, my son!
What is my life to me, now you are departed?

GENEVIEVE TAGGARD
To the Powers of Desolation

O mortal boy we cannot stop
The leak in that great wall where death seeps in
With hands or bodies, frantic mouths, or sleep.
Over the wall, over the wall's top
I have seen rising waters, waters of desolation.

From my despair bibles are written, children begotten;
Women open the wrong doors; men lie in ditches retching—
The horrible bright eyes of insanity fix on a blue fly,
Focus, enlarge. Dear mortal, escape
You cannot. I hear the drip of eternity above the quiet buzz
        of your sleep.
The waters are pouring, boiling over the wall; at the door
Where murder is under way they fall knocking on silence.
Go, that we may not hunger any more,
Or repeat again the wild ritual, the pang;
I will lie face downward
In an oblivion of waters,
Weeping in no way except in these words,
Caring then for nothing; for the blue wasp in the dabble of
        blood, perhaps, only,
While the slow waters pour.

ANONYMOUS

Bury Me Not on the Lone Prairie

"O bury me not on the lone prairie!"
These words came low and mournfully
From the pallid lips of a youth who lay
On his dying bed at the close of day.

"O bury me not on the lone prairie,
Where the wild coyotes will howl o'er me,
Where the buzzards beat and the wind goes free;
O bury me not on the lone prairie!

"O bury me not on the lone prairie,
In a narrow grave six foot by three,
Where the buffalo paws o'er a prairie sea;
O bury me not on the lone prairie!

"O bury me not on the lone prairie,
Where the wild coyotes will howl o'er me,
Where the rattlesnakes hiss and the crow flies free;
O bury me not on the lone prairie!

"O bury me not," and his voice faltered there,
But we took no heed of his dying prayer;
In a narrow grave just six by three,
We buried him there on the lone prairie.

CARL SANDBURG
Cool Tombs

When Abraham Lincoln was shoveled into the tombs, he forgot
the copperheads and the assassin . . . in the dust, in
the cool tombs.

And Ulysses Grant lost all thought of con men and Wall Street,
cash and collateral turned ashes . . . in the dust, in
the cool tombs.

Pocahontas' body, lovely as a poplar, sweet as a red haw in
November or a pawpaw in May, did she wonder? does
she remember? . . . in the dust, in the cool tombs?

Take any streetful of people buying clothes and groceries,
cheering a hero or throwing confetti and blowing tin
horns . . . tell me if the lovers are losers . . . tell me
if any get more than the lovers . . . in the dust . . .
in the cool tombs.

VACHEL LINDSAY

The Eagle That Is Forgotten

*(John P. Altgeld, b. December 30, 1847;
d. March 12, 1902)*

Sleep softly . . . eagle forgotten . . . under the stone.
Time has its way with you there, and the clay has its own.

"We have buried him now," thought your foes, and in secret
    rejoiced.
They made a brave show of their mourning, their hatred un-
    voiced.
They had snarled at you, barked at you, foamed at you day
    after day.
Now you were ended. They praised you, . . . and laid you
    away.

The others that mourned you in silence and terror and truth,
The widow bereft of her crust, and the boy without youth,
The mocked and the scorned and the wounded, the lame and
    the poor
That should have remembered forever, . . . remember no
    more.

Where are those lovers of yours, on what name do they call
The lost, that in armies wept over your funeral pall?
They call on the names of a hundred high-valiant ones,
A hundred white eagles have risen the sons of your sons,
The zeal in their wings is a zeal that your dreaming began
The valor that wore out your soul in the service of man.

Sleep softly, . . . eagle forgotten, . . . under the stone,
Time has its way with you there and the clay has its own.

Sleep on, O brave-hearted, O wise man, that kindled the
    flame—
To live in mankind is far more than to live in a name,
To live in mankind, far, far more . . . than to live in a name.

BOB KAUFMAN
Benediction

Pale brown Moses went down to Egypt land
To let somebody's people go.
Keep him out of Florida, no UN there:
The poor governor is all alone,
With six hundred thousand illiterates.

America, I forgive you . . . I forgive you
Nailing black Jesus to an imported cross
Every six weeks in Dawson, Georgia.
America, I forgive you . . . I forgive you
Eating black children, I know your hunger.
America, I forgive you . . . I forgive you
Burning Japanese babies defensively—
I realize how necessary it was.
Your ancestor had beautiful thoughts in his brain.
His descendants are experts in real estate.
Your generals have mushrooming visions.
Everyday your people get more and more
Cars, televisions, sickness, death dreams.
You must have been great
Alive.

ANCA VRBOVSKA
The Dream Is a Cradle

The dream is a cradle
rocked by Death's slowest hand.
Swing me, swing me,
gently sing me,
for the angels soon to ring me
into God's cash register.

In his palm, what a coin—
where will he toss me?
Slip me into his
breast pocket,
a souvenir to keep me?
Like Aaron's rod, Jacob's ladder,
the basket of little Moses,
or Mary Magdalene's roses,
and her hair, rose-scented hair
that wiped Jesus' feet?

Greetings to all
in a locket,
that God, the dreamer,
God, the lover,
has forgotten,
yet keeps forever
in his breast pocket.

ROBERT BLY

Hurrying Away from the Earth

The poor, and the dazed, and the idiots
Are with us, they live in the casket of the sun
And the moon's coffin, as I walked out tonight
Seeing the night wheeling their dark wheelbarrow
All about the plains of heaven,
And the stars inexorably rising.
Dark moon! Sinister tears!
Shadow of slums and of the conquering dead!

Some men have pierced the chest with a long needle
To stop their heart from beating any more;
Another put blocks of ice in his bed
So he would die, women
Have washed their hair, and hanged themselves
In the long braids, one woman climbed
A high elm above her lawn,
Opened a box, and swallowed poisonous spiders. . . .

The time for exhortation is past. I have heard
The iron chairs scraping in asylums,
As the cold bird hunches into the winter
In the windy night of November.
The coal miners rise from their pits
Like a flash flood,
Like a rice field disintegrating.
Men cry when they hear stories of someone rising from the
     dead.

168

EMILY DICKINSON
If I Should Die
No. 54

If I should die,
And you should live—
And time should gurgle on—
And morn should beam—
And noon should burn—
As it has usual done—
If Birds should build as early
and Bees as bustling go—
One might depart at option
From enterprise below!
'Tis sweet to know that stocks will stand
When we with Daisies lie—
That Commerce will continue—
And Trades as briskly fly—
It makes the parting tranquil
And keeps the soul serene—
That gentlemen so sprightly
Conduct the pleasing scene!

WHICH SIDE ARE YOU ON?

MRS. SAM REECE
Which Side Are You On?

They say in Harlan County
There are no neutrals there;
You either are a union man
Or a thug for J. H. Blair.

>Which side are you on?
>Which side are you on?

Oh workers, can you stand it?
Oh tell me how you can.
Will you be a lousy scab
Or will you be a man?

>Which side are you on?
>Which side are you on?

My daddy was a miner,
He is now in the air and sun
He'll be with you fellow workers
Until the battle's won.

>Which side are you on?
>Which side are you on?

NAOMI REPLANSKY
A Good Day's Work

Whose dog am I?
The time clock's dog.
Whose dog are you?

Learn how to smile at foremen.
A dirty joke and time for a smoke.
Be slick, be quick, be human.

The night is small
And hard to hold,
Sinks into the spongy morning.
The day is large
And hard to pass
And I can't go over it
And can't go under it
And can't go around it
But must go through it.

And me dogtired.

MICHAEL GOLD

A Strange Funeral in Braddock

Listen to the mournful drums of a strange funeral.
Listen to the story of a strange American funeral.

In the town of Braddock, Pennsylvania,
Where steel mills live like foul dragons, burning, devouring
    man and earth and sky,
It is spring. Now the spring has wandered in, a frightened
    child in the land of the steel ogres,
And Jan Clepak, the great grinning Bohemian, on his way
    to work at six in the morning,
Sees buttons of bright grass on the hills across the river, and
    plum trees hung with wild white blossoms,
And as he sweats half-naked at his puddling trough, a fiend
    by the lake of brimstone,
The plum trees soften his heart,
The green grass-memories return and soften his heart,
And he forgets to be hard as steel and remembers only his
    wife's breasts, his baby's little laughters and the way
    men sing when they are happy,
He remembers cows and sheep, and the grinning peasants,
    and the villages and fields of sunny Bohemia.

Listen to the mournful drums of a strange funeral.
Listen to the story of a strange American funeral.

Wake up, wake up! Jan Clepak, the furnaces are roaring like
    tigers,
The flames are flinging themselves at the high roof, like mad,
    yellow tigers at their cage,

Wake up! it is ten o'clock, and the next batch of mad,
　　flowing steel is to be poured into your puddling trough,
Wake up! Wake up! for a flawed lever is cracking in one of
　　those fiendish cauldrons,
Wake up! and wake up! for now the lever has cracked, and
　　the steel is raging and running down the floor like an
　　escaped madman,
Wake up! Oh, the dream is ended, and the steel has swallowed
　　you forever, Jan Clepak!

Listen to the mournful drums of a strange funeral.
Listen to the story of a strange American funeral.

Now three tons of hard steel hold at their heart the bones,
　　flesh, nerves, the muscles, brains and heart of Jan Clepak,
They hold the memories of green grass and sheep, the plum
　　trees, the baby-laughter, and the sunny Bohemian
　　villages.
And the directors of the steel mill present the great coffin
　　of steel and man-memories to the widow of Jan Clepak,
And on a great truck it is borne now to the great trench in
　　the graveyard,
And Jan Clepak's widow and two friends ride in a carriage
　　behind the block of steel that holds Jan Clepak,
And they weep behind the carriage blinds, and mourn the
　　soft man who was slain by hard steel.

Listen to the mournful drums of a strange funeral.
Listen to the story of a strange American funeral.

Now three thinkers are thinking strange thoughts in the
　　graveyard.
"O, I'll get drunk and stay drunk forever, I'll never marry
　　woman, or father laughing children,
I'll forget everything, I'll be nothing from now on,
Life is a dirty joke, like Jan's funeral!"

One of the friends is thinking in the sweet-smelling
    graveyard,
As a derrick lowers the three tons of steel that held Jan
    Clepak.
(LISTEN TO THE DRUMS OF THE STRANGE
    AMERICAN FUNERAL!)

"I'll wash clothes, I'll scrub floors, but my children will never
    work in the steel mill!"
Jan Clepak's wife is thinking as earth is shoveled over the
    great steel coffin,
In the spring sunlight, in the soft April air,
(LISTEN TO THE DRUMS OF THE STRANGE
    AMERICAN FUNERAL!)

"I'll make myself hard as steel, harder,
I'll come some day and make bullets of Jan's body, and
    shoot them into a tyrant's heart!"
The other friend is thinking, the listener,
He who listened to the mournful drums of the strange
    funeral,
Who listened to the story of the strange American funeral,
And turned as mad as a fiendish cauldron with cracked lever.

LISTEN TO THE MOURNFUL DRUMS OF A STRANGE
    FUNERAL.
LISTEN TO THE STORY OF A STRANGE AMERICAN
    FUNERAL.

ARCHIBALD MACLEISH
Burying Ground by the Ties

Ayee! Ai! This is heavy earth on our shoulders:
There were none of us born to be buried in this earth:
Niggers we were, Portuguese, Magyars, Polacks:

We were born to another look of the sky certainly.
Now we lie here in the river pastures:
We lie in the mowings under the thick turf:

We hear the earth and the all-day rasp of the grasshoppers.
It was we laid the steel to this land from ocean to ocean:
It was we (if you know) put the U.P. through the passes

Bringing her down into Laramie full load,
Eighteen mile on the granite anticlinal,
Forty-three foot to the mile and the grade holding:

It was we did it: hunkies of our kind.
It was we dug the caved-in holes for the cold water:
It was we built the gully spurs and the freight sidings:

Who would do it but we and the Irishmen bossing us?
It was all foreign-born men there were in this country:
It was Scotsmen, Englishmen, Chinese, Squareheads,
    Austrians . . .

Ayee! but there's weight to the earth under it.
Not for this did we come out—to be lying here
Nameless under the ties in the clay cuts:

There's nothing good in the world but the rich will buy it:
Everything sticks to the grease of a gold note—
Even a continent—even a new sky!

Do not pity us much for the strange grass over us:
We laid the steel to the stone stock of these mountains:
The place of our graves is marked by the telegraph poles!

It was not to lie in the bottoms we came out
And the trains going over us here in the dry hollows . . .

ALFRED KREYMBORG
Monotone

To this thin man in gray
pierced by the wintry wind
with many a Christian nail,
one thing is faithful: poverty.

To these rejected bones
blown like inhuman leaves,
nothing is true that was true
before: nothing but poverty.

To that low hat in hand,
depraved and frozen glance,
nobody pays a shiver or
gives his bread away.

On that infernal sore
and scarecrow of the race,
echo closes every door
and hide our wealth away.

Into that wretched wraith
hugged by the heavenly air,
God drives a nail, the faithful
breath and death of poverty.

EDWIN MARKHAM
From The Man with the Hoe

Bowed by the weight of centuries he leans
Upon his hoe and gazes on the ground,
The emptiness of ages in his face,
And on his back the burden of the world.
Who made him dead to rapture and despair,
A thing that grieves not and that never hopes,
Stolid and stunned, a brother to the ox?
Who loosened and let down this brutal jaw?
Whose was the hand that slanted back this brow?
Whose breath blew out the light within this brain? . . .

O masters, lords and rulers in all lands,
How will the Future reckon with this man?
How answer his brute question in that hour
When whirlwinds of rebellion shake all shores?
How will it be with kingdoms and with kings—
With those who shaped him to the thing he is—
When this dumb terror shall rise to judge the world,
After the silence of the centuries?

WOODY GUTHRIE
Hard Travelin'

I've been doing some hard traveling, I thought you knowed,
I've been doing some hard rambling, way down the road,
For I've been doing some hard rambling, hard drinking, hard
    gambling,
I've been doing some hard traveling, Lord.

I've been doing some hardrock mining, I thought you knowed,
I've been leaning on a pressure drill way down the road.
Well, the hammer flying and the air hose sucking,
And six feet of mud and I sure been a-mucking.
And I've been doing some hard traveling, Lord.

I've been laying in a hardrock jail, I thought you knowed, boys,
I've been laying out ninety days, way down the road,
Well, the darned old judge he said to me,
It's ninety days for vagrancy,
And I've been doing some hard traveling, Lord.

I've been riding them fast passengers, I thought you knowed,
    boys,
I've been hitting them flat wheelers, way down the road,
I've been riding them blind passengers,
Dead enders, picking up cinders,
I've been doing some hard traveling, Lord.

I've been doing some hard harvesting, I thought you knowed,
From North Dakota to Kansas City, way down the road,
Been a-cutting that wheat and a-stacking that hay.
Just trying to make about a dollar a day,
And I've been doing some hard traveling, Lord.

I've been walking that Lincoln Highway, I thought you
        knowed,
I've been hitting that '66', way down the road,
Got a heavy load, I got a worried mind,
I'm looking for a woman that's hard to find,
And I've been doing some hard traveling, Lord.

ANONYMOUS
John Henry

John Henry told his old captain,
Said, "A man ain't nothin' but a man;
Before I let your steel gang down
I will die with the hammer in my hand."

John Henry told his captain,
"Next time you go to town
Uh-jes' bring me back a ten-pound maul
For to beat your steel-drivin' down."

John Henry sez to his shaker:
"Brother, why don' you sing?
I'm throwin' twelve poun' from my hips on down,
Jes' lissen to de col' steel ring."

John Henry went down de railroad
Wid a twelve-poun' hammer by his side,
He walked down de track but he didn' come back,
Cause he laid down his hammer an' he died.

John Henry hammered in de mountains,
De mountains wuz so high.
De las' words I heard de pore boy say:
"Gimme a cool drink o' watah fo' I die."

John Henry had a little baby,
Hel' him in de palm of his han'
De las' words I heard de pore boy say:
"Son, yo're gonna be a steel-drivin' man."

ARTURO GIOVANNITTI

From When the Cock Crows

To the memory of Frank Little hanged at midnight

Six men drove up to his house at midnight, and woke
    the poor woman who kept it,
And asked her: "Where is the man who spoke against
    war and insulted the Army?"

And the old woman took fear of the men and the hour,
    and showed them the room where he slept,
And when they made sure it was he whom they wanted,
    they dragged him out of his bed with blows, though
    he was willing to walk,
And they fastened his hands on his back, and they drove
    him across the black night. . . .
And they drew the noose around his neck, and they
    pulled him up to the trestle, and they watched him
    until he was dead,
Six masked men whose faces were eaten with the cancer
    of the dark,
One for each steeple of thy temples, O Labor.
And even though you smite me with your bludgeon
    upon my head,
And curse me and call me foul names, and spit on my
    face and on my bare hands,
I swear that when the cock crows I shall not deny him.
And even if the power of your lie be so strong that
    my own mother curse me as a traitor with her hands
    clutched over her old breasts,
And my daughters with the almighty names turn their
    faces from me and call me coward.

And the One whose love for me is a battle flag in the
storm, scream for the shame of me and abjure my
name,
I swear that when the cock crows I shall not deny
him.
And if you chain me and drag me before the Beast that
guards the seals of your power, and the caitiff that
conspired against the daylight demand of my death.
And your hangman throw a black cowl over my head
and tie a noose around my neck,
And the black ghoul that pastures on the graves of the
saints digs its snout into my soul and howls the terrors
of the everlasting beyond in my ears,
Even then, when the cock crows, I swear I shall not
deny him.
And if you spring the trap under my feet and hurl me
into the gloom, and in the revelation of that instant
eternal a voice shriek madly to me
That the rope is forever unbreakable.
That the dawn is never to blaze,
That the night is forever invincible,
Even then, even then, O Monsters, I shall not deny
him.

STERLING BROWN

Strong Men

The strong men keep coming on.—Sandburg.

They dragged you from homeland,
They chained you in coffles,
They huddled you spoon-fashion in filthy hatches,
They sold you to give a few gentlemen ease.

They broke you in like oxen,
They scourged you,
They branded you,
They made your women breeders,
They swelled your numbers with bastards . . .
They taught you the religion they disgraced.

You sang:
     Keep a-inchin' along
     Lak a po' inch worm . . .

You sang:
     Bye and bye
     I'm gonna lay down this heavy load . . .

You sang:
     Walk togedder, chillen,
     Dontcha git weary . . .

       The strong men keep a-comin' on
       The strong men git stronger.
They point with pride to the roads you built for them,
They ride in comfort over the rails you laid for them.
They put hammers in your hands
And said—Drive so much before sundown.

You sang:

> Ain't no hammah
> In dis lan'
> Strikes lak mine, bebby,
> Strikes lak mine.

They cooped you in their kitchens,
They penned you in their factories,
They gave you the jobs that they were too good for,
They tried to guarantee happiness to themselves
By shunting dirt and misery to you.

You sang:

> Me an' muh baby gonna shine, shine
> Me an' muh baby gonna shine.
>> The strong men keep a'comin' on
> The strong men git stronger . . .

They bought off some of your leaders
You stumbled, as blind men will . . .
They coaxed you, unwontedly soft-voiced . . .
You followed a way.
They laughed as usual.
They heard the laugh and wondered;
Uncomfortable;
Unadmitting a deeper terror . . .

> The strong men keep a'comin' on
> Gittin' stronger . . .

What, from the slums
Where they have hemmed you,
What, from the tiny huts
They could not keep from you—
What reaches them
Making them ill at ease, fearful?
Today they shout prohibition at you
"Thou shalt not this"

"Thou shalt not that"
"Reserved for whites only"
You laugh.

One thing they cannot prohibit—
      The strong men . . . coming on
      The strong men gittin' stronger.
      Strong men . . .
      Stronger . . .

Walter Lowenfels, a native New Yorker, was one of the expatriate poets in the Paris of the '20s and '30s when Henry Miller called him "probably *the* poet of the age." Then he stopped writing, returned to the United States, and only resumed publishing in the past decade.

In addition to his own poems, Lowenfels is the author of *Walt Whitman's Civil War* and several popular anthologies including *Poets of Today* and *Where Is Vietnam?*

He lives with his wife, Lillian, in Peekskill, New York. They have four daughters and twelve grandchildren, so that his prose book *To an Imaginary Daughter* has a certain basis of reality to it.